Who Is on the Lord's Side? A Call to Righteousness

Joshua Rhoades

Published by Joshua Paul Rhoades, 2024.

WHO IS ON THE LORD'S SIDE? A CALL TO RIGHTEOUSNESS

First edition. August 22, 2024.

Copyright © 2024 Joshua Rhoades.

ISBN: 979-8227426062

Written by Joshua Rhoades.

Also by Joshua Rhoades

Courage Under Fire: David's Stand On The Battlefield
Jonah's Journey: Voices Of Redemption And Lessons In Obedience
The Furnace Of Faith: 12 Principles From The Heat Of Faith
Whispers of Hope: Inspiring Stories of Men's Prayers In Scripture
Frontier Legends: The Oregon Dream
Elijah: A Beacon Of Boldness
HOOK, LINE & SAVIOUR - Faith Reflections from Fishing
Driven By Faith: Motor Racing Inspired Christian Life
30 Day Devotional - Bold and Strong- Coffee Devotions for a
Courageous Christian Walk
Authentic Christianity: The Heart of Old Time Religion
Consider The Ant - God's Tiny Preachers
Flee Fornication: The Plea For Purity
Renewed Hope- How to Find Encouragement in God
Sounding The Call - The Voice of Conviction
The Altar - Where Heaven Meets Earth
The Bible's Battlefields- Timeless Lessons from Ancient Wars
The Sacred Art of Silence - How Silence Speaks in Scripture
Under Fire- The Sanctity of the Traditional Biblical Home
Who Is on the Lord's Side? A Call to Righteousness

Introduction

In a world increasingly marked by moral confusion and spiritual complacency, the question posed by Moses thousands of years ago, "Who is on the Lord's side?" resonates more urgently than ever. In an age where the lines between right and wrong are often blurred, and where societal pressures encourage compromise rather than conviction, there is a profound need for leaders who are willing to stand firm, lead with integrity, and call others to a life of righteousness. This book, "Who Is on the Lord's Side? A Call to Righteousness," seeks to provide a framework for understanding how to navigate the spiritual and moral challenges of our time, drawing from the timeless principles illustrated in the life of Moses.

The story of Moses standing at the gate of the camp and challenging the Israelites to declare their allegiance is more than just a historical account; it is a call to action that reverberates through the ages. Moses was faced with a rebellious and disobedient people, much like we encounter today in various forms. Yet, he did not shrink back from his responsibility. Instead, he stood firm, relying on his deep relationship with God to guide him in making difficult decisions that would restore the people to righteousness. His leadership was not based on personal power or charisma, but on a profound commitment to justice, righteousness, and the authority of God.

This book explores the twelve principles drawn from Moses' leadership during this pivotal moment, principles that are as relevant now as they were in his time. These principles—such as bold leadership in crisis, unwavering commitment to God, the courage to stand alone, and a passion for God's glory—serve as a guide for anyone who seeks to lead others in a manner that honors God. Whether you are a pastor, a parent, a teacher, or simply someone striving to live out your faith in a challenging world, these principles will equip you to stand firm in your convictions and to inspire others to do the same.

"Who Is on the Lord's Side? A Call to Righteousness" is not just a manual for leadership; it is a call to every believer to examine their own life, to assess where they stand in their relationship with God, and to make the necessary changes to align their life with His will. In a time when the world desperately needs voices of truth and leaders of integrity, this book is a reminder that we are all called to be on the Lord's side, to stand for what is right, and to lead others into the light of God's righteousness.

As you read through the pages of this book, may you be challenged, inspired, and equipped to take your stand for the Lord. The journey of leading and standing firm in faith is not an easy one, but it is a journey worth taking. The question remains: Who is on the Lord's side? The time to answer is now.

Chapter 1- Pivotal Leadership in Crisis

Moses stood at the gate of the camp, and his voice rang out with a firmness that demanded attention. This was no ordinary day; this was a day of crisis, a day when the people of Israel had turned their backs on the God who had rescued them from the bondage of Egypt. They had forgotten the miraculous parting of the Red Sea, the manna from heaven, the water from the rock. Instead, they had crafted a golden calf and bowed down to worship it, declaring it their god. Moses, having been on Mount Sinai communing with God, returned to find the people lost in idolatry and sin. The scene was one of chaos, with the people dancing and celebrating around the idol they had made, a stark betrayal of the God who had brought them so far. It was in this moment of widespread rebellion that Moses showed what it means to be a bold leader in a time of crisis. Moses could have responded in many ways. He could have joined the people, rationalizing that it was easier to go along with the crowd. He could have turned his back on them in anger, leaving them to their fate. But Moses was not an ordinary man; he was a leader chosen by God, and he understood the gravity of the situation. The people were on the brink of destroying the covenant they had made with God, and something had to be done to bring them back to their senses. So, Moses stood firm. He did not waver or hesitate; he did not let fear or doubt cloud his judgment. Instead, he took decisive action, breaking the stone tablets inscribed with the Ten Commandments, a symbol of the broken covenant between God and Israel. This was not a rash or impulsive act; it was a bold statement that things could not continue as they were. The people needed to understand the seriousness of their sin and the consequences it would bring.

Moses then stood at the gate of the camp and called out, "Who is on the Lord's side? Let him come unto me." This was a call to action, a demand for the people to choose where they stood. In times of crisis, a leader must be able to make the hard decisions and call others to do the same. Moses knew that the people needed to be brought back to their senses, and he was willing to stand alone if necessary to make that happen. His leadership was not about seeking popularity or approval; it was about doing what was right, even when it was difficult. This is the essence of bold leadership in crisis: the ability to stand firm in the face of widespread rebellion and to take action that others might fear or avoid.

The people of Israel were in a state of moral confusion, and it was Moses' role to bring clarity and order. He did this not by softening the truth or offering easy solutions but by confronting the problem head-on. Bold leadership requires the courage to speak the truth, even when it is uncomfortable or unpopular. Moses did not shy away from telling the people that they were wrong, that they had sinned against God, and that they needed to repent. This was not a message that the people wanted to hear, but it was the message they needed to hear. In times of crisis, a leader must be willing to deliver the hard truths, to challenge the status quo, and to lead others in a new direction, even if it means standing alone.

Moses' leadership was not just about words; it was about action. After calling the people to choose sides, Moses took further action to restore order and bring the people back to God. He instructed the Levites to go through the camp and execute judgment on those who persisted in their rebellion. This was a harsh and difficult task, but it was necessary to purify the camp and restore the people to a right relationship with God. Bold leadership in crisis requires the willingness to take difficult actions, even when they are painful. Moses understood that the future of the nation depended on their faithfulness to God, and he was willing to do whatever it took to bring them back to that faithfulness.

In addition to taking decisive action, Moses also demonstrated the importance of intercession in leadership. After confronting the people and taking action to restore order, Moses returned to the mountain to plead with God on behalf of the Israelites. He understood that the people had sinned greatly and that they deserved God's judgment, but he also knew that God was merciful and forgiving. Moses interceded for the people, asking God to forgive them and to continue to be with them as they journeyed to the Promised Land. This act of intercession shows that bold leadership in crisis is not just about taking action but also about seeking God's guidance and mercy. A true leader understands that they cannot lead on their own strength but must rely on God's wisdom and grace.

Moses' actions in this crisis also show the importance of accountability in leadership. He held the people accountable for their actions, making it clear that there were consequences for their rebellion. But he also held himself accountable, acknowledging that as their leader, he bore some responsibility for their actions. This is an important aspect of bold leadership in crisis: the willingness to take responsibility for the actions of those you lead and to seek forgiveness and restoration. Moses did not try to shift the blame or make excuses; he stood before God and the people as a leader who was fully committed to doing what was right, even when it was difficult.

Another key aspect of Moses' leadership in this crisis was his ability to remain calm and focused under pressure. The situation in the camp was chaotic, with the people engaged in all kinds of sinful behavior. It would have been easy for Moses to become overwhelmed or to react out of anger or frustration. But Moses remained calm and focused, understanding that his role as a leader was to bring order and to guide the people back to God. Bold leadership in crisis requires the ability to stay calm and focused, to keep your eye on the goal, and to take the necessary steps to achieve it, even in the midst of chaos and confusion. Moses' leadership also demonstrated the importance of perseverance. The crisis in the camp was not resolved in a single moment; it required sustained effort and determination. Moses did not give up or lose heart, even when the situation seemed hopeless. He continued to lead the people with patience and determination, guiding them step by step back to a right relationship with God. This perseverance is a crucial aspect of bold leadership in crisis. It is not enough to take decisive action in the moment; a leader must be willing to stay the course, to keep working toward the goal, even when the going gets tough.

In conclusion, the moment when Moses stood at the gate of the camp and called out, "Who is on the Lord's side? Let him come unto me," is a powerful example of bold leadership in crisis. Moses' actions in this moment show us what it means to be a strong leader in times of rebellion and moral confusion. He stood firm in the face of widespread sin, took decisive action to restore order, and called the people to make a clear choice. He spoke the truth, even when it was difficult, and he took the necessary steps to bring the people back to God. He demonstrated the importance of intercession, accountability, calmness, focus, and perseverance in leadership. Moses was not afraid to stand alone, to take a bold stand for what was right, and to lead the people back to a right relationship with God. His leadership in this crisis is a model for all who are called to lead in difficult times, showing us that bold leadership requires courage, conviction, and a deep commitment to doing what is right, no matter the cost.

Chapter 2 - Persistent Commitment to God

Moses is one of the most significant figures in the Bible, and his story, particularly in the book of Exodus, teaches us many valuable lessons about leadership, faith, and commitment. One of the most important lessons we learn from Moses is his unwavering commitment to God, even in the face of immense pressure and widespread disobedience among the people he was leading. This is especially evident in the story of the golden calf, which is found in Exodus 32. The Israelites, whom Moses had led out of slavery in Egypt, had grown impatient while waiting for Moses to return from Mount Sinai, where he was meeting with God. In their impatience, they turned to Aaron, Moses' brother, and demanded that he make them a god to worship. Aaron, unfortunately, gave in to their demands and created a golden calf, which the people then began to worship. This was a direct violation of the first two commandments that God had given them, and it was an act of great disobedience. When Moses came down from the mountain and saw what the people were doing, he was furious. However, despite the pressure he faced from the people and the overwhelming tide of disobedience around him, Moses remained steadfast in his commitment to God. This story exemplifies the need for unwavering loyalty to the Lord, even when it seems like everyone else has turned away.

Moses' unwavering commitment to God is evident in the way he responded to the situation. When he saw the people worshipping the golden calf, he didn't hesitate to take action. He knew that what they were doing was wrong, and he wasn't afraid to stand up for what was right, even if it meant standing alone. This is a powerful example of what it means to be committed to God. In our own lives, we will face situations where we are tempted to go along with the crowd, even when we know it's not the right thing to do. However, if we are truly committed to God, we must be willing to stand up for what is right, even if it means standing alone. This can be difficult, especially when we are facing pressure from others to conform, but Moses' example shows us that it is possible to remain steadfast in our faith, even in the face of immense pressure.

One of the reasons Moses was able to remain so committed to God is because he had a deep and personal relationship with Him. Throughout the book of Exodus, we see numerous examples of Moses spending time with God, seeking His guidance, and relying on His strength. Moses didn't try to lead the people on his own; he knew that he needed God's help and direction. This is a crucial lesson for all of us. If we want to remain committed to God, we need to spend time with Him, seek His guidance, and rely on His strength. It's easy to get caught up in the busyness of life and to neglect our relationship with God, but if we want to stay faithful to Him, we must make our relationship with Him a priority. Moses' commitment to God was not just something he professed with his words; it was something he lived out in his actions. He didn't just say he was committed to God; he showed it by the way he lived his life.

Another important aspect of Moses' unwavering commitment to God is his willingness to confront sin. When he saw the people worshipping the golden calf, he didn't ignore it or try to make excuses for their behavior. Instead, he confronted them about their sin and took decisive action to address the situation. This is another powerful lesson for us. If we are truly committed to God, we can't turn a blind eye to sin, whether it's in our own lives or in the lives of those around us. We need to be willing to confront sin and take the necessary steps to address it. This can be uncomfortable and difficult, but it's an important part of staying faithful to God. Moses' example shows us that true commitment to God involves not only standing up for what is right but also being willing to confront and deal with sin. Moses' commitment to God also involved a deep sense of responsibility for the people he was leading. Even though the people had sinned greatly, Moses didn't abandon them or wash his hands of the situation. Instead, he interceded for them before God, pleading for their forgiveness. This shows us that true commitment to God involves a deep love and concern for others. It's not just about our own personal relationship with God; it's also about caring for those around us and seeking their well-being. Moses' willingness to intercede for the people, even after they had sinned, is a powerful example of the kind of selfless love and commitment that God calls us to have.

Moses' unwavering commitment to God also involved a willingness to stand firm, even when faced with opposition. When he came down from the mountain and confronted the people about their sin, he didn't back down or try to soften the message. He stood firm in his conviction that what they were doing was wrong, and he called them to repentance. This is an important lesson for us as well. If we are truly committed to God, we need to be willing to stand firm in our convictions, even when it's difficult or unpopular. This can be challenging, especially in a world that often values compromise and conformity, but Moses' example shows us that it's possible to stand firm in our faith, even in the face of opposition.

Another aspect of Moses' unwavering commitment to God is his humility. Despite being chosen by God to lead the people of Israel, Moses never let his position go to his head. He remained humble and recognized that his ability to lead came from God, not from his own strength or abilities. This humility is an important aspect of true commitment to God. It's easy to become prideful or self-reliant, especially when we experience success or recognition. However, if we want to remain faithful to God, we must stay humble and recognize that everything we have and everything we are comes from Him. Moses' humility is a powerful reminder that true commitment to God involves recognizing our dependence on Him and giving Him the glory for all that we accomplish.

Moses' commitment to God also involved a deep sense of obedience. Throughout his life, Moses was obedient to God's commands, even when they were difficult or didn't make sense to him. Whether it was leading the people out of Egypt, crossing the Red Sea, or wandering in the wilderness for forty years, Moses trusted God and followed His instructions. This obedience is a key aspect of true commitment to God. It's easy to be obedient when things are going well or when we understand what God is asking us to do. But true commitment to God involves being obedient even when it's difficult or when we don't fully understand His plan. Moses' obedience is a powerful example of what it means to be truly committed to God.

In addition to obedience, Moses' commitment to God also involved a willingness to sacrifice. Throughout his life, Moses made many sacrifices in order to follow God and lead the people of Israel. He gave up a life of comfort and privilege in Egypt to follow God's call. He endured criticism, opposition, and hardship in order to fulfill God's plan. This willingness to sacrifice is an important aspect of true commitment to God. Following God often requires us to give up our own desires, plans, and comforts in order to follow His will. Moses' willingness to sacrifice is a powerful reminder that true commitment to God involves being willing to give up whatever is necessary in order to follow Him.

Moses' unwavering commitment to God also involved a deep sense of perseverance. Leading the people of Israel was not an easy task. They were often disobedient, rebellious, and ungrateful. They complained and grumbled, and they frequently questioned Moses' leadership. However, despite all of these challenges, Moses never gave up. He continued to lead the people with patience and determination, even when the going was tough. This perseverance is a crucial aspect of true commitment to God. It's easy to be committed when things are going well, but true commitment is tested when we face difficulties and challenges. Moses' perseverance is a powerful example of what it means to be truly committed to God, even in the face of adversity.

Moses' unwavering commitment to God also had a profound impact on the people he was leading. His example of faithfulness and obedience inspired others to follow God as well. This is an important reminder that our commitment to God is not just about us; it also has an impact on those around us. When we remain steadfast in our faith, even in the face of challenges, we inspire others to do the same. Moses' example shows us that true commitment to God is not just about our own personal relationship with Him; it's also about influencing and inspiring others to follow Him as well.

In conclusion, Moses' unwavering commitment to God is a powerful example of what it means to be truly faithful. Despite the pressure and the tide of disobedience around him, Moses remained steadfast in his faith and in his commitment to God. He was willing to stand up for what was right, even if it meant standing alone. He was willing to confront sin and take decisive action to address it. He was willing to take responsibility for the people he was leading and to intercede for them before God. He was willing to stand firm in his convictions, even in the face of opposition. He remained humble, obedient, and willing to sacrifice in order to follow God's will. And he persevered, even in the face of great challenges and difficulties. Moses' example shows us that true commitment to God involves all of these things and more. It involves a deep and personal relationship with God, a willingness to stand up for what is right, a commitment to confronting and dealing with sin, a willingness to take responsibility for others, and a determination to remain faithful, even in the face of challenges. Moses' unwavering commitment to God is a powerful reminder of what it means to be truly faithful, and it challenges all of us to examine our own lives and to strive to live with the same level of commitment and faithfulness.

Chapter 3 - Precise Call to Righteousness

In the story of Moses and the golden calf, found in Exodus 32, we see a powerful example of what it means to issue a clear call to righteousness in times of moral confusion. The Israelites, who had been delivered from slavery in Egypt by the mighty hand of God, found themselves in a state of moral confusion while waiting for Moses to return from Mount Sinai, where he was receiving the Ten Commandments from God. Impatient and unsure of what had become of Moses, the people turned to Aaron, Moses' brother, and demanded that he make them a god to worship. Aaron, perhaps out of fear or a desire to appease the people, gave in to their demands and created a golden calf, which the people then worshipped, declaring it to be their god. This act was a direct violation of the commandments that God had given them, particularly the commandment to have no other gods before Him and to make no graven images. The people had fallen into idolatry, a grave sin that threatened to sever their relationship with God.

When Moses came down from the mountain and saw what the people were doing, he was filled with righteous anger. He immediately recognized the seriousness of the situation and knew that something had to be done to bring the people back to their senses. In that moment of crisis, Moses stood at the gate of the camp and called out in a loud voice, "Who is on the Lord's side? Let him come unto me." This was a clear and uncompromising call to righteousness. Moses was not interested in finding a middle ground or making compromises with sin. He was not concerned with being politically correct or avoiding offending anyone. His primary concern was with doing what was right in the eyes of God and leading the people back to a right relationship with Him. This is the essence of a clear call to righteousness: it is a call that is rooted in a deep commitment to God and an unwavering commitment to His standards of right and wrong.

Moses' call to righteousness was clear because it demanded a response. It was not a vague or ambiguous statement; it required the people to make a choice. They had to decide whether they were going to continue in their sin and idolatry or whether they were going to turn back to God and recommit themselves to following His commandments. This is an important aspect of a clear call to righteousness: it requires people to take action. It is not enough to simply acknowledge that something is wrong; there must be a willingness to turn away from that wrong and to do what is right. Moses understood this, and that is why his call to the people was so direct and uncompromising. He did not leave room for negotiation or debate; he simply called the people to make a choice and to take a stand. In issuing this call to righteousness, Moses demonstrated the importance of leadership in times of moral confusion. When the people were lost and unsure of what to do, they needed someone to step forward and guide them back to the right path. Moses did just that. He did not wait for someone else to take the lead or hope that the people would come to their senses on their own. He took decisive action and called the people to make a choice. This is what true leadership looks like: it is the willingness to stand up and speak the truth, even when it is difficult or unpopular. It is the courage to call people to a higher standard and to hold them accountable to that standard. In times of moral confusion, clear and decisive leadership is essential, and Moses provided that leadership in a powerful way.

Moses' call to righteousness was also an act of love. Although he was angry with the people for their sin, his call to them was motivated by a desire to see them restored to a right relationship with God. He knew that their idolatry was leading them down a path of destruction, and he wanted to bring them back before it was too late. This is another important aspect of a clear call to righteousness: it is not about condemnation or judgment; it is about love and restoration. When we call others to righteousness, it should be out of a desire to see them experience the fullness of life that comes from living in accordance with God's will. Moses' actions show us that a true call to righteousness is rooted in a deep love for God and for others.

The clarity of Moses' call to righteousness is also seen in the way he addressed the sin of the people. He did not try to minimize or excuse their behavior; he confronted it head-on. He recognized the seriousness of their idolatry and took immediate action to address it. He broke the stone tablets on which the Ten Commandments were written, a symbolic act that demonstrated the breaking of the covenant between God and the people. He then ground the golden calf into powder, scattered it on the water, and made the people drink it. This was a clear and dramatic way of showing the people the consequences of their sin. Moses' actions were not intended to be punitive but to bring the people to a place of repentance. He knew that they needed to see the seriousness of their sin in order to truly turn away from it and return to God. This is an important lesson for us: when we issue a call to righteousness, we must be clear about the consequences of sin. People need to understand that sin has real and serious consequences, and they need to be called to repentance in a way that is clear and uncompromising.

Moses' call to righteousness also required the people to take responsibility for their actions. By calling them to choose sides, he was asking them to take ownership of their sin and to make a conscious decision to turn away from it. This is another important aspect of a clear call to righteousness: it requires people to take responsibility for their actions. It is not enough to simply acknowledge that something is wrong; there must be a willingness to take responsibility for it and to make a change. Moses understood this, and that is why his call to the people was so powerful. He was not content to let them continue in their sin; he wanted them to take responsibility for it and to make a conscious decision to turn back to God.

In addition to calling the people to take responsibility for their actions, Moses' call to righteousness also emphasized the need for accountability. By asking the people to come to him if they were on the Lord's side, he was holding them accountable for their actions. He was making it clear that there were consequences for their sin and that they needed to take steps to make things right. This kind of accountability is essential in any call to righteousness. People need to know that their actions have consequences, and they need to be held accountable for their behavior. Moses' example shows us that true leadership involves holding people accountable to the standards that God has set for us.

Moses' call to righteousness also required the people to make a public commitment. By asking them to come to him if they were on the Lord's side, he was asking them to make a public declaration of their faith. This public commitment is an important aspect of our relationship with God. It is not enough to simply believe in God in our hearts; we need to be willing to make a public declaration of our faith and to live in a way that honors God. Moses' call to the people is a reminder that true faith requires us to make a clear and public commitment to God, and to live in a way that reflects that commitment.

Moses' call to righteousness was also a call to unity. By asking the people to come to him if they were on the Lord's side, he was bringing them together around a common goal: returning to God and living in a way that honored Him. This unity is essential in any spiritual community. When we are united in our commitment to God and to living in a way that honors Him, we are stronger and more effective in our mission. Moses' example shows us that true leadership involves bringing people together around a common goal and helping them to work together to achieve that goal.

Moses' call to righteousness also emphasized the need for a clear and uncompromising stand against sin. By asking the people to come to him if they were on the Lord's side, Moses was making it clear that there was no room for compromise when it came to sin. This is an important aspect of spiritual leadership. We cannot afford to be wishy-washy or indecisive when it comes to matters of righteousness. We need to be willing to take a clear and uncompromising stand against sin, and to call others to do the same. Moses' example shows us that true leadership involves taking a clear and uncompromising stand against sin, and helping others to do the same.

Moses' call to righteousness also highlighted the importance of repentance. By asking the people to come to him if they were on the Lord's side, he was inviting them to repent of their sin and to return to God. Repentance is an essential part of the Christian life. It involves recognizing our sins, feeling genuine sorrow for them, and making a commitment to turn away from them and live a life that is pleasing to God. Moses' call to the people is a reminder that no matter how far we may have strayed, there is always a way back to God. But that way back requires us to make a clear and decisive choice to turn away from our sin and to stand with the Lord.

Moses' call to righteousness also required the people to take immediate action. By calling them to come to him, he was asking them to make a decision right then and there. This urgency is an important aspect of a clear call to righteousness. When we are confronted with sin, we need to take immediate action to address it. We cannot afford to wait or delay; we need to make a decision to turn away from sin and to turn back to God right away. Moses understood this, and that is why his call to the people was so urgent. He knew that they needed to take action immediately in order to be restored to a right relationship with God.

Moses' call to righteousness also emphasized the importance of obedience. By asking the people to come to him if they were on the Lord's side, he was calling them to obey God's commandments. This obedience is a key aspect of true commitment to God. It's easy to be obedient when things are going well or when we understand what

God is asking us to do. But true commitment to God involves being obedient even when it's difficult or when we don't fully understand His plan. Moses' call to the people is a reminder that true obedience requires us to trust in God's plan and to follow His commandments, even when it's difficult.

Moses' call to righteousness also involved a willingness to sacrifice. By asking the people to come to him if they were on the Lord's side, he was asking them to give up their idolatry and to make sacrifices in order to follow God. This willingness to sacrifice is an important aspect of true commitment to God. Following God often requires us to give up our own desires, plans, and comforts in order to follow His will. Moses' call to the people is a reminder that true commitment to God involves being willing to give up whatever is necessary in order to follow Him.

Moses' call to righteousness also involved a deep sense of perseverance. Leading the people of Israel was not an easy task. They were often disobedient, rebellious, and ungrateful. They complained and grumbled, and they frequently questioned Moses' leadership. However, despite all of these challenges, Moses never gave up. He continued to lead the people with patience and determination, even when the going was tough. This perseverance is a crucial aspect of true commitment to God. It's easy to be committed when things are going well, but true commitment is tested when we face difficulties and challenges. Moses' perseverance is a powerful example of what it means to be truly committed to God, even in the face of adversity.

Moses' call to righteousness also had a profound impact on the people he was leading. His example of faithfulness and obedience inspired others to follow God as well. This is an important reminder that our commitment to God is not just about us; it also has an impact on those around us. When we remain steadfast in our faith, even in the face of challenges, we inspire others to do the same. Moses' example shows us that true commitment to God is not just about our own personal relationship with Him; it's also about influencing and inspiring others to follow Him as well.

In conclusion, Moses' clear call to righteousness in Exodus 32 is a powerful example of what it means to stand firm in the face of moral confusion and to lead others back to a right relationship with God. His call was clear, uncompromising, and rooted in a deep love for God and for the people he was leading. It required the people to take responsibility for their actions, to make a public commitment, and to take immediate action to turn away from their sin and return to God. Moses' example shows us that true leadership involves issuing a clear and uncompromising call to righteousness, holding people accountable to God's standards, and leading them with love, courage, and perseverance. His call to the people of Israel is a timeless reminder of the importance of standing firm in our faith, even in times of moral confusion, and of leading others back to a right relationship with God.

Chapter 4 - Purification from Sin

In the story of Moses and the golden calf in Exodus 32, we see a powerful and crucial lesson about the need for separation from sin. Moses, who had been chosen by God to lead the Israelites out of slavery in Egypt and into the Promised Land, went up Mount Sinai to receive the Ten Commandments from God. While Moses was on the mountain, the people grew restless and impatient, and they demanded that Aaron, Moses' brother, make them a god that they could worship. Aaron, perhaps out of fear or a desire to please the people, gave in to their demands and fashioned a golden calf out of their jewelry. The people then began to worship the golden calf, declaring it to be the god that had brought them out of Egypt. This act was a blatant act of idolatry and a direct violation of the first two commandments that God had given them: to have no other gods before Him and to make no graven images. When Moses came down from the mountain and saw what the people were doing, he was filled with righteous anger. He immediately recognized the gravity of their sin and knew that something had to be done to bring them back to God. In that moment, Moses stood at the gate of the camp and called out, "Who is on the Lord's side? Let him come unto me." This was not just a call to rally the people; it was a call to separate themselves from sin and idolatry and to choose holiness over compromise.

Moses' call to the people to stand with the Lord was a clear and uncompromising call to separate themselves from the sin that had taken hold of their camp. It was a call to make a choice between continuing in their idolatry and turning back to the one true God who had delivered them from Egypt. This moment in the history of the Israelites highlights the importance of separating ourselves from sin and choosing to live a life of holiness. Sin, by its very nature, separates us from God, and if we want to live in a right relationship with Him, we must be willing to separate ourselves from the things that lead us away from Him. Moses understood this, and that is why his call to the people was so direct and uncompromising. He knew that they could not continue to worship the golden calf and still be in a right relationship with God. They had to make a choice: to either turn away from their sin and idolatry or face the consequences of their actions.

The need for separation from sin is a theme that runs throughout the Bible. From the very beginning, when Adam and Eve sinned in the Garden of Eden, we see that sin creates a separation between humanity and God. This separation is not just a physical separation, but a spiritual one as well. Sin corrupts our hearts and minds, and it leads us away from the holiness that God desires for us. In order to be in a right relationship with God, we must be willing to separate ourselves from sin and choose to live a life that is pleasing to Him. This is not always easy, especially in a world that often encourages us to compromise our values and to go along with the crowd. But as followers of God, we are called to a higher standard. We are called to be holy, just as God is holy.

Moses' call to the people to stand with the Lord was also a call to repentance. By asking the people to come to him if they were on the Lord's side, Moses was inviting them to turn away from their sin and to recommit themselves to God. Repentance is a crucial part of our relationship with God. It involves recognizing our sin, feeling genuine sorrow for it, and making a commitment to turn away from it and to live in a way that is pleasing to God. Moses understood that in order for the people to be restored to a right relationship with God, they needed to repent of their idolatry and to separate themselves from the sin that had taken hold of their lives. This is an important lesson for us as well. In our own lives, we must be willing to repent of our sins and to separate ourselves from the things that lead us away from God. This may mean making difficult choices or giving up things that we enjoy, but if we want to live in a right relationship with God, we must be willing to do whatever it takes to separate ourselves from sin.

Moses' call to the people also emphasized the importance of making a clear and decisive choice. By asking the people to come to him if they were on the Lord's side, he was asking them to make a public declaration of their commitment to God. This was not something that could be done half-heartedly or in secret. It required the people to take a stand and to make a clear choice about where their loyalties lay. This is an important aspect of separating ourselves from sin. We cannot afford to be wishy-washy or indecisive when it comes to matters of righteousness. We must be willing to take a clear and uncompromising stand against sin and to declare our allegiance to God. This may mean going against the crowd or standing alone, but if we want to live a life that is pleasing to God, we must be willing to do whatever it takes to separate ourselves from sin and to choose holiness.

Moses' actions in this moment also demonstrate the importance of accountability in our relationship with God. By calling the people to separate themselves from their sin, Moses was holding them accountable for their actions. He was making it clear that there were consequences for their idolatry and that they needed to take responsibility for their behavior. This is an important aspect of separating ourselves from sin. We must be willing to take responsibility for our actions and to hold ourselves accountable to the standards that God has set for us. This may mean confessing our sins to God and to others, seeking forgiveness, and making restitution for the wrongs that we have done. But if we want to live a life that is pleasing to God, we must be willing to hold ourselves accountable and to take the necessary steps to separate ourselves from sin.

Moses' call to the people also emphasized the importance of community in our relationship with God. By asking the people to come to him if they were on the Lord's side, Moses was bringing them together around a common goal: to return to God and to live a life that was pleasing to Him. This unity was essential in helping the people to separate themselves from their sin and to recommit themselves to God.

In our own lives, we need the support and encouragement of others to help us separate ourselves from sin and to live a life of holiness. This is why it is so important to be a part of a community of believers who can hold us accountable, encourage us, and pray for us as we seek to live a life that is pleasing to God.

Moses' call to the people also required them to take immediate action. By calling them to come to him, he was asking them to make a decision right then and there. This urgency is an important aspect of separating ourselves from sin. When we are confronted with sin in our lives, we need to take immediate action to address it. We cannot afford to wait or delay; we need to make a decision to turn away from sin and to turn back to God right away. Moses understood this, and that is why his call to the people was so urgent. He knew that they needed to take action immediately in order to be restored to a right relationship with God.

Moses' call to the people also emphasized the importance of obedience. By asking the people to come to him if they were on the Lord's side, he was calling them to obey God's commandments. This obedience is a key aspect of separating ourselves from sin. It's easy to be obedient when things are going well or when we understand what God is asking us to do. But true obedience requires us to trust in God's plan and to follow His commandments, even when it's difficult or when we don't fully understand what He is asking us to do. Moses' call to the people is a reminder that true obedience requires us to trust in God and to follow His commandments, even when it means separating ourselves from things that we may want or enjoy.

Moses' call to the people also required them to make sacrifices. By asking them to come to him if they were on the Lord's side, he was asking them to give up their idolatry and to make sacrifices in order to follow God. This willingness to sacrifice is an important aspect of separating ourselves from sin. Following God often requires us to give up our own desires, plans, and comforts in order to follow His will. Moses' call to the people is a reminder that true commitment to God involves being willing to give up whatever is necessary in order to separate ourselves from sin and to live a life that is pleasing to Him.

Moses' call to the people also involved a deep sense of perseverance. Leading the people of Israel was not an easy task. They were often disobedient, rebellious, and ungrateful. They complained and grumbled, and they frequently questioned Moses' leadership. However, despite all of these challenges, Moses never gave up. He continued to lead the people with patience and determination, even when the going was tough. This perseverance is a crucial aspect of separating ourselves from sin. It's easy to be committed when things are going well, but true commitment is tested when we face difficulties and challenges. Moses' perseverance is a powerful example of what it means to be truly committed to separating ourselves from sin and to living a life that is pleasing to God, even in the face of adversity.

Moses' call to the people also had a profound impact on the people he was leading. His example of faithfulness and obedience inspired others to follow God as well. This is an important reminder that our commitment to separating ourselves from sin is not just about us; it also has an impact on those around us. When we remain steadfast in our faith, even in the face of challenges, we inspire others to do the same. Moses' example shows us that true commitment to God is not just about our own personal relationship with Him; it's also about influencing and inspiring others to separate themselves from sin and to follow Him as well.

In conclusion, Moses' call to the people to separate themselves from sin and idolatry in Exodus 32 is a powerful example of what it means to choose holiness over compromise. His call was clear, uncompromising, and rooted in a deep love for God and for the people he was leading. It required the people to take responsibility for their actions, to make a public commitment, and to take immediate action to turn away from their sin and return to God. Moses' example shows us that true leadership involves issuing a clear and uncompromising call to righteousness, holding people accountable to God's standards, and leading them with love, courage, and perseverance. His call to the people of Israel is a timeless reminder of the importance of separating ourselves from sin, choosing holiness over compromise, and leading others to do the same. In our own lives, we must be willing to make the difficult choices and sacrifices that are necessary to separate ourselves from the things that lead us away from God and to live a life that is pleasing to Him. Moses' example challenges all of us to examine our own lives and to strive to live with the same level of commitment and faithfulness, choosing holiness over compromise, and leading others to do the same.

Chapter 5 - Providing Guidance for God's People

Moses is one of the most important figures in the Bible, and his life is filled with lessons about leadership, faith, and responsibility. One of the most powerful examples of his leadership is found in Exodus 32, when the people of Israel fell into idolatry by worshiping a golden calf while Moses was on Mount Sinai receiving the Ten Commandments from God. This moment was a major crisis for the Israelites, and it required strong and decisive leadership to bring the people back to God. When Moses came down from the mountain and saw what the people were doing, he was filled with righteous anger. He knew that the people had sinned greatly against God and that something had to be done to restore them to the right path. Instead of abandoning the people or letting them continue in their sin, Moses took responsibility for guiding them back to God. He stood at the gate of the camp and called out, "Who is on the Lord's side? Let him come unto me." This was not just a call to rally the people; it was an act of leadership that demonstrated Moses' commitment to taking responsibility for God's people and guiding them back to the right path. This moment highlights the role of a leader in spiritual restoration and the importance of taking responsibility for the well-being of others, especially in times of crisis.

Moses' decision to stand at the gate and call the people to him was a clear and decisive action that showed his understanding of the gravity of the situation. The people had fallen into idolatry, a sin that threatened to sever their relationship with God, and Moses knew that this was a moment that required strong leadership. He didn't wait for someone else to take action or hope that the situation would resolve itself. Instead, he took it upon himself to address the problem and guide the people back to the right path. This is a powerful example of what it means to take responsibility for others, especially in a spiritual context. As a leader, Moses understood that his role was not just to lead the people in the good times, but also to guide them back to God when they went astray. This is a crucial aspect of spiritual leadership: the willingness to take responsibility for the spiritual well-being of others and to take action when they are in danger of losing their way.

Moses' actions in this moment also demonstrate the importance of accountability in leadership. By calling the people to him, Moses was holding them accountable for their actions. He was making it clear that there were consequences for their idolatry and that they needed to take responsibility for their behavior. This is an important aspect of leadership, especially in a spiritual context. As leaders, we must be willing to hold others accountable for their actions and to guide them back to the right path when they go astray. This is not always an easy task, but it is a necessary one if we are to fulfill our responsibilities as leaders. Moses' example shows us that true leadership involves holding people accountable to God's standards and guiding them back to the right path when they go astray.

In addition to holding the people accountable, Moses' actions in this moment also demonstrate the importance of intercession in leadership. After calling the people to him, Moses went back up the mountain to intercede for them before God. He pleaded with God to forgive the people for their sin and to continue to be with them as they journeyed to the Promised Land. This act of intercession shows that Moses understood the importance of seeking God's guidance and mercy on behalf of the people. As leaders, we must be willing to intercede for those we lead, seeking God's forgiveness and guidance for them when they go astray. This is a crucial aspect of spiritual leadership: the willingness to stand in the gap for others and to seek God's mercy and guidance on their behalf.

Moses' actions in this moment also demonstrate the importance of humility in leadership. Despite being chosen by God to lead the people of Israel, Moses did not let his position go to his head. Instead, he remained humble and recognized that his ability to lead came from God, not from his own strength or abilities. This humility is an important aspect of true leadership, especially in a spiritual context. It is easy to become prideful or self-reliant, especially when we experience success or recognition. However, if we want to be effective leaders, we must stay humble and recognize that everything we have and everything we are comes from God. Moses' humility in this moment is a powerful reminder that true leadership involves recognizing our dependence on God and giving Him the glory for all that we accomplish.

Moses' actions in this moment also demonstrate the importance of perseverance in leadership. Leading the people of Israel was not an easy task. They were often disobedient, rebellious, and ungrateful. They complained and grumbled, and they frequently questioned Moses' leadership. However, despite all of these challenges, Moses never gave up. He continued to lead the people with patience and determination, even when the going was tough. This perseverance is a crucial aspect of true leadership. It is easy to be committed when things are going well, but true commitment is tested when we face difficulties and challenges.

Moses' perseverance is a powerful example of what it means to be truly committed to leading others, even in the face of adversity.

Moses' actions in this moment also demonstrate the importance of leading by example. When Moses called the people to stand with the Lord, he was not just giving them a command; he was setting an example for them to follow. He demonstrated his own commitment to God by taking a stand and calling others to do the same. This is an important aspect of leadership: the willingness to lead by example and to demonstrate through our actions what it means to be committed to God. As leaders, we must be willing to set an example for others to follow, showing them through our own lives what it means to live in a way that is pleasing to God.

Moses' actions in this moment also demonstrate the importance of making difficult decisions in leadership. By calling the people to separate themselves from their sin, Moses was asking them to make a difficult choice. He was asking them to turn away from their idolatry and to recommit themselves to God. This was not an easy decision for the people to make, but it was a necessary one if they were to be restored to a right relationship with God. As leaders, we must be willing to guide others in making difficult decisions, even when those decisions are painful or challenging. This is a crucial aspect of leadership: the willingness to guide others in making the right choices, even when those choices are difficult.

Moses' actions in this moment also demonstrate the importance of taking responsibility for the spiritual well-being of others. By calling the people to him and guiding them back to God, Moses was taking responsibility for their spiritual restoration. He understood that as their leader, it was his responsibility to guide them back to the right path when they went astray. This is an important aspect of spiritual leadership: the willingness to take responsibility for the spiritual well-being of others and to guide them back to God when they are in danger of losing their way.

Moses' actions in this moment also demonstrate the importance of compassion in leadership. Despite the people's sin, Moses did not abandon them or give up on them. Instead, he took responsibility for their spiritual restoration and interceded for them before God. This act of compassion shows that true leadership involves caring for others and seeking their well-being, even when they have gone astray. As leaders, we must be willing to show compassion to those we lead, seeking their well-being and guiding them back to God when they are in danger of losing their way.

Moses' actions in this moment also demonstrate the importance of faith in leadership. Despite the people's sin, Moses had faith that God would forgive them and restore them to a right relationship with Him. This faith is an important aspect of true leadership, especially in a spiritual context. It is easy to lose faith when things go wrong or when those we lead go astray. However, if we want to be effective leaders, we must have faith that God is in control and that He will guide us and those we lead back to the right path.

Moses' actions in this moment also demonstrate the importance of trust in leadership. Despite the people's sin, Moses trusted that God would forgive them and restore them to a right relationship with Him. This trust is an important aspect of true leadership, especially in a spiritual context. It is easy to lose trust when things go wrong or when those we lead go astray. However, if we want to be effective leaders, we must trust that God is in control and that He will guide us and those we lead back to the right path.

Moses' actions in this moment also demonstrate the importance of forgiveness in leadership. Despite the people's sin, Moses sought God's forgiveness on their behalf. This act of forgiveness shows that true leadership involves seeking and extending forgiveness to others, even when they have gone astray. As leaders, we must be willing to seek forgiveness for those we lead and to extend forgiveness to them when they repent and seek to return to the right path.

Moses' actions in this moment also demonstrate the importance of hope in leadership. Despite the people's sin, Moses had hope that God would forgive them and restore them to a right relationship with Him. This hope is an important aspect of true leadership, especially in a spiritual context. It is easy to lose hope when things go wrong or when those we lead go astray. However, if we want to be effective leaders, we must have hope that God is in control and that He will guide us and those we lead back to the right path.

Moses' actions in this moment also demonstrate the importance of love in leadership. Despite the people's sin, Moses loved them enough to take responsibility for their spiritual restoration and to intercede for them before God. This act of love shows that true leadership involves caring for others and seeking their well-being, even when they have gone astray. As leaders, we must be willing to show love to those we lead, seeking their well-being and guiding them back to God when they are in danger of losing their way.

Moses' actions in this moment also demonstrate the importance of wisdom in leadership. Despite the people's sin, Moses used wisdom in guiding them back to the right path. He understood the importance of addressing their sin and guiding them back to God in a way that was both firm and compassionate. This wisdom is an important aspect of true leadership, especially in a spiritual context. It is easy to react out of anger or frustration when those we lead go astray. However, if we want to be effective leaders, we must use wisdom in guiding others back to the right path, addressing their sin in a way that is both firm and compassionate.

Moses' actions in this moment also demonstrate the importance of courage in leadership. Despite the people's sin, Moses had the courage to stand up and take responsibility for their spiritual restoration. This courage is an important aspect of true leadership, especially in a spiritual context. It is easy to shrink back or avoid taking responsibility when those we lead go astray. However, if we want to be effective leaders, we must have the courage to take responsibility for the spiritual well-being of others and to guide them back to the right path.

Moses' actions in this moment also demonstrate the importance of integrity in leadership. Despite the people's sin, Moses maintained his integrity by taking responsibility for their spiritual restoration and guiding them back to God. This integrity is an important aspect of true leadership, especially in a spiritual context. It is easy to compromise our values or avoid taking responsibility when those we lead go astray. However, if we want to be effective leaders, we must maintain our integrity by taking responsibility for the spiritual well-being of others and guiding them back to the right path.

Moses' actions in this moment also demonstrate the importance of patience in leadership. Despite the people's sin, Moses showed patience in guiding them back to the right path. He understood that spiritual restoration is a process that takes time and requires patience. This patience is an important aspect of true leadership, especially in a spiritual context. It is easy to become impatient or frustrated when those we lead go astray. However, if we want to be effective leaders, we must show patience in guiding others back to the right path, understanding that spiritual restoration is a process that takes time.

Moses' actions in this moment also demonstrate the importance of perseverance in leadership. Despite the people's sin, Moses persevered in guiding them back to the right path. He did not give up on them, even when the going was tough. This perseverance is an important aspect of true leadership, especially in a spiritual context. It is easy to give up or lose heart when those we lead go astray. However, if we want to be effective leaders, we must persevere in guiding others back to the right path, even when the going is tough.

In conclusion, Moses' actions in Exodus 32, when he stood at the gate of the camp and called the people to him, are a powerful example of what it means to take responsibility for God's people and guide them back to the right path. His actions demonstrate the importance of accountability, intercession, humility, perseverance, leading by example, making difficult decisions, taking responsibility for others, showing compassion, having faith and trust in God, seeking forgiveness, maintaining hope, showing love, using wisdom, having courage, maintaining integrity, showing patience, and persevering in leadership. These qualities are essential for true leadership, especially in a spiritual context. Moses' example challenges all of us to examine our own lives and to strive to be leaders who take responsibility for the spiritual well-being of others and guide them back to the right path, even in the face of adversity.

Chapter 6 - Principled Moral Courage

Moses is one of the most significant figures in the Bible, and his life is filled with lessons about leadership, faith, and the courage it takes to do what is right, even when it is difficult. One of the most powerful examples of this courage is found in the story of the golden calf in Exodus 32. The people of Israel, whom Moses had led out of slavery in Egypt, had become impatient while waiting for Moses to return from Mount Sinai, where he was receiving the Ten Commandments from God. In their impatience, they turned to Aaron, Moses' brother, and demanded that he make them a god to worship. Aaron, perhaps out of fear or a desire to please the people, gave in to their demands and created a golden calf, which the people then worshipped, declaring it to be the god that had brought them out of Egypt. This act of idolatry was a direct violation of the first two commandments that God had given them, and it was a serious sin that threatened to destroy the covenant between God and the Israelites. When Moses came down from the mountain and saw what the people were doing, he was filled with righteous anger. But more importantly, he displayed moral courage by confronting the people's sin directly, rather than avoiding the difficult truth of what they had done.

Moses could have chosen to ignore the situation, hoping that it would resolve itself, or he could have tried to find a way to excuse the people's behavior. After all, they had been through a lot, and they were undoubtedly scared and confused. But Moses knew that sin, especially the sin of idolatry, could not be ignored or excused. It had to be confronted head-on, no matter how difficult or uncomfortable that might be. This is what moral courage is all about: the willingness to face wrongdoing directly, even when it would be easier to look the other way or to pretend that everything is okay. Moses understood that the only way to truly address the situation was to confront it directly, to call out the sin for what it was, and to take action to correct it.

When Moses came down from the mountain and saw the golden calf, he immediately took action. He didn't hesitate or try to find a way to soften the blow. He broke the stone tablets on which the Ten Commandments were written, symbolizing the breaking of the covenant between God and the people. He then ground the golden calf into powder, scattered it on the water, and made the people drink it. This was a dramatic and powerful way of showing the people the seriousness of their sin. Moses' actions were not intended to be punitive or vindictive; rather, they were a way of bringing the people to a place of repentance. He knew that the only way for the people to be restored to a right relationship with God was for them to fully understand the gravity of what they had done and to turn away from their sin. This is an important aspect of moral courage: the willingness to take action, even when it is difficult, in order to bring about the best possible outcome for those involved. Moses' confrontation of the people's sin also highlights the importance of speaking the truth, even when it is uncomfortable. It would have been much easier for Moses to come down from the mountain and try to find a way to smooth things over, to tell the people that everything would be okay and that they just needed to try harder next time. But Moses knew that this was not the truth, and he was not willing to compromise the truth for the sake of making people feel better. Instead, he told the people the hard truth: that they had sinned against God and that there were serious consequences for their actions. This is a crucial aspect of moral courage: the willingness to speak the truth, even when it is difficult or unpopular, and even when it might cause discomfort or pain. Moses understood that the truth, even when it is hard to hear, is always better than a comforting lie. By confronting the people's sin directly and speaking the truth about what they had done, Moses was able to lead them to a place of repentance and restoration.

Another important aspect of moral courage that Moses demonstrated is the willingness to stand alone, if necessary, in order to do what is right. When Moses confronted the people about their sin, he was not concerned with whether or not they would agree with him or whether they would continue to follow him. He was only concerned with doing what was right in the eyes of God. This is an important lesson for all of us: sometimes, doing what is right means standing alone, going against the crowd, and being willing to face criticism or rejection. Moses was willing to take that stand, even if it meant losing the support of the people he had led out of Egypt. This kind of moral courage is rare, but it is essential for true leadership. Moses understood that his first loyalty was to God, not to the opinions or approval of others. This is what allowed him to take such a bold and uncompromising stand in the face of the people's sin.

Moses' actions in this moment also demonstrate the importance of accountability in leadership. By confronting the people's sin directly, Moses was holding them accountable for their actions. He was making it clear that there were consequences for their behavior and that they needed to take responsibility for what they had done. This is an important aspect of moral courage: the willingness to hold others accountable, even when it is difficult or uncomfortable. As leaders, we must be willing to confront wrongdoing and to hold others accountable for their actions, even when it might strain relationships or cause conflict. This is not about being harsh or punitive; rather, it is about helping others to grow and to learn from their mistakes. Moses understood that accountability is a crucial part of leadership, and he was willing to take on that responsibility, even when it was difficult.

Moses' confrontation of the people's sin also highlights the importance of repentance in the process of spiritual restoration. By confronting the people's sin directly and taking decisive action to address it, Moses was leading them to a place of repentance. He understood that true repentance requires more than just feeling sorry for what we have done; it requires a complete turning away from sin and a commitment to live differently in the future. This is an important aspect of moral courage: the willingness to confront sin in a way that leads to genuine repentance and transformation. Moses knew that the people needed to fully understand the seriousness of their sin in order to truly repent and be restored to a right relationship with God. This is why he took such bold and decisive action, even though it was difficult and painful.

Moses' actions in this moment also demonstrate the importance of humility in leadership. Despite being chosen by God to lead the people of Israel, Moses did not let his position or authority go to his head. Instead, he remained humble and focused on doing what was right in the eyes of God. This humility is an important aspect of moral courage: the willingness to put aside our own pride or ego in order to do what is right. Moses understood that his role as a leader was not about seeking power or recognition for himself, but about serving God and guiding the people in the way that they should go. This is what allowed him to take such a bold and courageous stand in the face of the people's sin.

Moses' confrontation of the people's sin also highlights the importance of compassion in leadership. Although Moses was angry with the people for their sin, his actions were motivated by a deep love and concern for their well-being. He understood that their idolatry was leading them down a path of destruction, and he wanted to bring them back to God before it was too late. This is an important aspect of moral courage: the willingness to confront wrongdoing, not out of a desire to punish or condemn, but out of a genuine concern for the well-being of others. Moses' actions show us that true moral courage is rooted in love and compassion, and in a desire to see others restored to a right relationship with God.

Another important aspect of moral courage that Moses demonstrated is the willingness to take responsibility for the spiritual well-being of others. By confronting the people's sin and leading them to a place of repentance, Moses was taking responsibility for their spiritual restoration. He understood that as their leader, it was his responsibility to guide them back to the right path when they went astray. This is a crucial aspect of moral courage: the willingness to take responsibility for the well-being of others, even when it is difficult or challenging. Moses' actions in this moment show us that true leadership involves taking on the responsibility of guiding others back to God, even when it requires difficult and uncomfortable conversations.

Moses' confrontation of the people's sin also highlights the importance of perseverance in the face of adversity. The people of Israel were often disobedient, rebellious, and ungrateful, and they frequently questioned Moses' leadership. However, despite all of these challenges, Moses never gave up. He continued to lead the people with patience and determination, even when the going was tough. This perseverance is an important aspect of moral courage: the willingness to keep going, to keep doing what is right, even when it is difficult or when others are against us. Moses' perseverance in the face of the people's sin is a powerful example of what it means to have true moral courage.

Moses' actions in this moment also demonstrate the importance of faith in leadership. Despite the people's sin, Moses had faith that God would forgive them and restore them to a right relationship with Him. This faith is an important aspect of moral courage: the willingness to trust in God's goodness and mercy, even when the situation seems bleak. Moses understood that his role as a leader was not just to confront the people's sin, but also to guide them back to a place of faith and trust in God. This is what allowed him to take such a bold and courageous stand in the face of the people's sin.

Moses' confrontation of the people's sin also highlights the importance of integrity in leadership. Despite the pressure to go along with the crowd or to excuse the people's behavior, Moses maintained his integrity by confronting their sin directly and taking action to address it. This integrity is an important aspect of moral courage: the willingness to do what is right, even when it is difficult or unpopular.

Moses understood that true leadership requires a commitment to doing what is right, no matter the cost. This is what allowed him to take such a bold and courageous stand in the face of the people's sin.

Moses' actions in this moment also demonstrate the importance of accountability in leadership. By confronting the people's sin directly, Moses was holding them accountable for their actions. He was making it clear that there were consequences for their behavior and that they needed to take responsibility for what they had done. This is an important aspect of moral courage: the willingness to hold others accountable, even when it is difficult or uncomfortable. As leaders, we must be willing to confront wrongdoing and to hold others accountable for their actions, even when it might strain relationships or cause conflict. This is not about being harsh or punitive; rather, it is about helping others to grow and to learn from their mistakes. Moses understood that accountability is a crucial part of leadership, and he was willing to take on that responsibility, even when it was difficult.

Moses' confrontation of the people's sin also highlights the importance of humility in leadership. Despite being chosen by God to lead the people of Israel, Moses did not let his position go to his head. Instead, he remained humble and focused on doing what was right in the eyes of God. This humility is an important aspect of moral courage: the willingness to put aside our own pride or ego in order to do what is right. Moses understood that his role as a leader was not about seeking power or recognition for himself, but about serving God and guiding the people in the way that they should go. This is what allowed him to take such a bold and courageous stand in the face of the people's sin.

Moses' confrontation of the people's sin also highlights the importance of compassion in leadership. Although Moses was angry with the people for their sin, his actions were motivated by a deep love and concern for their well-being. He understood that their idolatry was leading them down a path of destruction, and he wanted to bring them back to God before it was too late. This is an important aspect of moral courage: the willingness to confront wrongdoing, not out of a desire to punish or condemn, but out of a genuine concern for the well-being of others. Moses' actions show us that true moral courage is rooted in love and compassion, and in a desire to see others restored to a right relationship with God. Another important aspect of moral courage that Moses demonstrated is the willingness to take responsibility for the spiritual well-being of others. By confronting the people's sin and leading them to a place of repentance, Moses was taking responsibility for their spiritual restoration. He understood that as their leader, it was his responsibility to guide them back to the right path when they went astray. This is a crucial aspect of moral courage: the willingness to take responsibility for the well-being of others, even when it is difficult or challenging. Moses' actions in this moment show us that true leadership involves taking on the responsibility of guiding others back to God, even when it requires difficult and uncomfortable conversations.

Moses' confrontation of the people's sin also highlights the importance of perseverance in the face of adversity. The people of Israel were often disobedient, rebellious, and ungrateful, and they frequently questioned Moses' leadership. However, despite all of these challenges, Moses never gave up. He continued to lead the people with patience and determination, even when the going was tough. This perseverance is an important aspect of moral courage: the willingness to keep going, to keep doing what is right, even when it is difficult or when others are against us. Moses' perseverance in the face of the people's sin is a powerful example of what it means to have true moral courage.

Moses' actions in this moment also demonstrate the importance of faith in leadership. Despite the people's sin, Moses had faith that God would forgive them and restore them to a right relationship with Him. This faith is an important aspect of moral courage: the willingness to trust in God's goodness and mercy, even when the situation seems bleak. Moses understood that his role as a leader was not just to confront the people's sin, but also to guide them back to a place of faith and trust in God. This is what allowed him to take such a bold and courageous stand in the face of the people's sin.

In conclusion, Moses' confrontation of the people's sin in Exodus 32 is a powerful example of moral courage. His actions demonstrate the importance of confronting wrongdoing directly, speaking the truth, holding others accountable, leading by example, taking responsibility for the well-being of others, showing compassion, maintaining humility, persevering in the face of adversity, and having faith in God's goodness and mercy. These qualities are essential for true leadership, especially in a spiritual context. Moses' example challenges all of us to examine our own lives and to strive to be leaders who display moral courage, even when it is difficult or unpopular. His actions show us that true moral courage is rooted in a deep commitment to doing what is right in the eyes of God, no matter the cost.

Chapter 7 - Passion for God's Glory

Moses is one of the most important figures in the Bible, and his life provides countless lessons about leadership, faith, and devotion to God. One of the most powerful lessons we can learn from Moses is his deep zeal for God's glory, which is evident in everything he did, especially during the challenging times when the people of Israel repeatedly tested God's patience. Moses was chosen by God to lead the Israelites out of slavery in Egypt and into the Promised Land, a task that required not only great courage and wisdom but also an unwavering commitment to God's honor and glory. This commitment is perhaps most strikingly displayed in the story of the golden calf in Exodus 32. While Moses was on Mount Sinai receiving the Ten Commandments from God, the people grew impatient and anxious in his absence. They pressured Aaron, Moses' brother, to make them a god that they could worship, leading Aaron to create a golden calf from the people's gold jewelry. The Israelites then began to worship this idol, declaring it to be the god that had brought them out of Egypt. This act of idolatry was a grave sin and a direct affront to the true God who had delivered them from bondage. When Moses came down from the mountain and saw what the people were doing, he was filled with righteous anger—not just because of the people's disobedience, but because of the deep dishonor they had shown to God. This reaction reveals Moses' deep zeal for God's glory, a driving force that shaped his leadership and defined his actions throughout his life.

Moses' zeal for God's glory is evident in the way he immediately took action to address the situation. He could have been tempted to downplay the severity of the people's actions or to seek a way to reconcile with them without causing too much conflict. However, Moses knew that the people's sin was not just a minor transgression—it was a direct insult to the God who had done so much for them. Moses understood that God's glory and honor were at stake, and he could not stand by and allow this offense to go unchallenged. In a dramatic display of his commitment to God's glory, Moses threw down the stone tablets on which the Ten Commandments were written, shattering them at the foot of the mountain. This act symbolized the breaking of the covenant between God and the people, a powerful statement that underscored the gravity of their sin. Moses' actions here were not motivated by personal anger or a desire for revenge; rather, they were driven by a deep concern for God's glory and honor. He wanted the people to understand that their actions had serious consequences and that they had deeply offended the God who had delivered them from slavery.

This zeal for God's glory is what made Moses such an effective leader. Throughout his life, Moses was consistently motivated by a desire to honor God and to make His name known among the people. He was not interested in gaining power or prestige for himself; his primary concern was that God's glory would be upheld and that the people would recognize and honor the true God. This is what true leadership looks like: a leader who is driven not by personal ambition or the desire for recognition, but by a deep and abiding passion for God's glory. Moses' actions in the face of the people's idolatry demonstrate this clearly. He was willing to take bold and decisive action, even when it was difficult, because he knew that God's honor was more important than anything else.

Moses' zeal for God's glory also drove him to intercede for the people when God's wrath was kindled against them. After seeing the golden calf and the people's sinful behavior, God told Moses that He was ready to destroy the Israelites and to start over with Moses, making him the father of a new nation. This was a significant offer—one that would have elevated Moses to an even higher status. However, Moses, in his deep concern for God's glory, pleaded with God to spare the people. He reminded God of His promises to Abraham, Isaac, and Jacob, and he argued that destroying the Israelites would bring dishonor to God's name among the nations. Moses was not concerned about his own status or legacy; his only concern was that God's name would be glorified and that His promises would be fulfilled. This selflessness is a key characteristic of true leadership: the willingness to put God's glory above one's own interests, even when it means making personal sacrifices.

Moses' intercession for the people is a powerful example of how his zeal for God's glory influenced every aspect of his leadership. He understood that the people's survival was not just about them—it was about God's reputation among the nations. Moses knew that if the Israelites were destroyed, the surrounding nations would question God's power and faithfulness. They would doubt whether the God of Israel was truly able to deliver on His promises. This was unacceptable to Moses, who could not bear the thought of God's name being dishonored. His plea to God was not based on the people's worthiness, but on the importance of upholding God's glory. This kind of leadership—one that is driven by a deep concern for God's glory rather than personal gain or recognition—is what set Moses apart and made him such an effective leader of God's people.

Moses' zeal for God's glory also influenced how he dealt with the people after their sin. He did not simply gloss over their wrongdoing or try to quickly move past it. Instead, he took the necessary steps to restore the people's relationship with God, even when those steps were difficult. After pleading with God to spare the people, Moses returned to the camp and took decisive action to address the sin that had been committed. He ordered the Levites to go through the camp and execute judgment on those who had refused to repent of their idolatry. This was a harsh and difficult task, but Moses knew it was necessary to cleanse the camp and restore the people's relationship with God. His actions here were not driven by a desire for vengeance, but by a deep concern for God's glory. He understood that the people's sin had to be dealt with seriously if they were to be restored to a right relationship with God and if God's glory was to be upheld among them.

Moses' actions also demonstrate that his zeal for God's glory was not just about confronting sin, but also about leading the people back to God in repentance and restoration. After dealing with the immediate consequences of the people's sin, Moses again went before God to plead for their forgiveness. He was willing to do whatever it took to restore the people to God, even offering to have his own name blotted out of God's book if it would save the Israelites. This self-sacrificial attitude is another key characteristic of true leadership: the willingness to lay down one's own life for the sake of others, all for the glory of God. Moses was not concerned with his own reputation or standing before God; he was only concerned with seeing the people restored to a right relationship with God and with ensuring that God's glory was upheld.

Moses' zeal for God's glory is a powerful example for us today. In a world where so many leaders are driven by a desire for power, recognition, and personal gain, Moses stands out as a leader who was driven by a deep and abiding passion for God's glory. His actions were motivated not by a desire to make a name for himself, but by a desire to honor God and to lead the people in doing the same. This is what true leadership looks like: a leader who is motivated by a deep concern for God's glory and who is willing to take bold and decisive action to uphold that glory, even when it is difficult or costly.

Moses' example also shows us that zeal for God's glory is not just about confronting sin or taking bold action—it is also about leading others to a deeper understanding and appreciation of God's greatness. Throughout his life, Moses consistently pointed the people back to God, reminding them of His power, His faithfulness, and His glory. He understood that the people's ultimate purpose was to glorify God, and he made it his mission to lead them in doing just that. Whether he was leading them through the Red Sea, bringing them the Ten

Commandments, or interceding for them before God, Moses was always focused on one thing: the glory of God. His life was a testament to the fact that true leadership is not about seeking glory for oneself, but about pointing others to the glory of God.

Moses' zeal for God's glory also influenced how he viewed his own role as a leader. He understood that his position as the leader of Israel was not about him, but about God. He was not interested in building his own legacy or making a name for himself; he was only concerned with fulfilling the mission that God had given him and with ensuring that God's glory was upheld. This humility is a key characteristic of true leadership. Moses understood that his role as a leader was not to seek his own glory, but to lead the people in glorifying God. This is what made him such an effective leader and what allowed him to accomplish so much for God's kingdom.

Moses' life is a powerful reminder that true leadership is driven by a deep concern for God's glory. Whether he was confronting the people's sin, interceding for them before God, or leading them through the wilderness, Moses was always motivated by a desire to see God's name honored and glorified. This zeal for God's glory is what made Moses such an effective leader and what set him apart as one of the greatest leaders in the Bible. His life challenges us to examine our own motivations and to ask ourselves whether we are driven by a desire for personal recognition or by a passion for God's glory. Moses' example shows us that true leadership is not about seeking glory for ourselves, but about pointing others to the glory of God.

In conclusion, Moses' life is a powerful example of what it means to have zeal for God's glory. His actions throughout his life were motivated by a deep concern for God's honor and a desire to see His name glorified among the people. Whether he was confronting sin, interceding for the people, or leading them through the wilderness, Moses was always focused on one thing: the glory of God. This is what made him such an effective leader and what set him apart as one of the greatest leaders in the Bible. Moses' life challenges us to examine our own motivations and to ask ourselves whether we are driven by a desire for personal recognition or by a passion for God's glory. His example shows us that true leadership is not about seeking glory for ourselves, but about pointing others to the glory of God. In a world where so many leaders are driven by a desire for power, recognition, and personal gain, Moses stands out as a leader who was driven by a deep and abiding passion for God's glory. His life is a testament to the fact that true leadership is about more than just leading people—it is about leading them to a deeper understanding and appreciation of God's greatness and ensuring that His name is honored and glorified in all that we do. Moses' zeal for God's glory is a powerful example for us to follow, and it challenges us to live our lives in such a way that we, too, are motivated by a deep concern for God's honor and a desire to see His name glorified in all that we do.

Chapter 8 - Perception of God's Will

Moses is a central figure in the Bible, and his life offers many lessons about leadership, faith, and the importance of following God's guidance. One of the most significant aspects of Moses' leadership was his ability to discern God's will, even in the most complex and challenging situations. This ability to understand and carry out God's will is especially evident in the story of the golden calf in Exodus 32. When Moses went up Mount Sinai to receive the Ten Commandments, the Israelites grew impatient and anxious. In Moses' absence, they pressured Aaron, his brother, to create a god that they could worship, leading to the creation of a golden calf. The people began to worship this idol, declaring it to be the god that had brought them out of Egypt. This act of idolatry was a grave sin and a direct violation of the first two commandments that God had given them. When Moses came down from the mountain and saw what the people were doing, he was faced with a complex and difficult situation. On one hand, he loved the people and had dedicated his life to leading them out of slavery and into the Promised Land. On the other hand, he knew that they had sinned against God in a serious way. In this moment, Moses needed to discern God's will and decide how to respond to the people's sin.

Moses' decision to draw a line between those who were for God and those who were against Him reflects the deep discernment he had in understanding and carrying out God's will. When he saw the people worshipping the golden calf, he knew that a clear and decisive action was needed to address the sin and restore the people to a right relationship with God. Moses did not hesitate or waver in his decision; he stood at the gate of the camp and called out, "Who is on the Lord's side? Let him come unto me." This was not just a call to rally the people; it was a decisive action that required the people to make a clear choice. They had to decide whether they would continue in their idolatry or turn back to God. Moses' decision to draw this line was an act of discernment, as he recognized that the people could not serve both the golden calf and the true God. He understood that the only way for the people to be restored to a right relationship with God was for them to separate themselves from their sin and recommit themselves to following God's commandments.

This moment highlights the importance of discernment in understanding and carrying out God's will. Moses was faced with a complex situation that required him to make a difficult decision. He could have chosen to overlook the people's sin or to try to find a compromise that would satisfy both God and the people. However, Moses understood that God's will required a clear and decisive action. He knew that the people's sin could not be ignored or excused and that they needed to make a clear choice about where their loyalties lay. This is an important lesson for all of us: in complex situations, we must seek to discern God's will and make decisions that are in line with His commands, even when those decisions are difficult or unpopular.

Moses' ability to discern God's will was not just about making the right decisions; it was also about understanding the deeper implications of those decisions. By drawing a line between those who were for God and those who were against Him, Moses was not just addressing the immediate issue of the golden calf; he was also setting a precedent for the people's relationship with God going forward. He understood that the people needed to be reminded of the seriousness of their covenant with God and that they could not serve both God and idols. This act of discernment went beyond just dealing with the immediate situation; it was about guiding the people in their ongoing relationship with God. Moses recognized that their relationship with God required them to make a clear and unwavering commitment to Him and that this commitment could not be compromised by idolatry or sin.

This ability to discern God's will is a key aspect of spiritual leadership. As leaders, we are often faced with complex and challenging situations that require us to make difficult decisions. In these moments, it is essential that we seek to understand God's will and make decisions that are in line with His commands. This requires us to be in tune with God's Spirit, to seek His guidance in prayer, and to be willing to take bold and decisive action when necessary. Moses' example shows us that true leadership is not about making decisions based on what is easy or popular; it is about seeking to discern God's will and acting in accordance with it, even when it is difficult or unpopular.

Moses' discernment of God's will also required him to take responsibility for the consequences of his decisions. After drawing the line between those who were for God and those who were against Him, Moses took further action to address the sin in the camp. He ordered the Levites to go through the camp and execute judgment on those who had refused to repent of their idolatry. This was a harsh and difficult task, but Moses knew that it was necessary to restore the people's relationship with God. This willingness to take responsibility for the consequences of his decisions is another key aspect of discernment. It is not enough to simply make the right decision; we must also be willing to take responsibility for the outcomes of those decisions and to follow through on the actions that are necessary to carry out God's will.

Moses' ability to discern God's will also required him to be sensitive to the needs and concerns of the people he was leading. While he took bold and decisive action to address the sin in the camp, he also showed compassion and concern for the people's well-being. After dealing with the immediate consequences of their sin, Moses again went before God to plead for their forgiveness. He was willing to stand in the gap for the people, even offering to have his own name blotted out of God's book if it would save the Israelites. This willingness to intercede for the people and to seek God's mercy on their behalf is a crucial aspect of discernment. It shows that true discernment is not just about making tough decisions; it is also about caring for the people we are leading and seeking their well-being, even when they have gone astray.

Moses' discernment of God's will also involved a deep understanding of the importance of God's honor and glory. When God threatened to destroy the Israelites and start over with Moses, making him the father of a new nation, Moses could have easily accepted this offer and elevated his own status. However, Moses was more concerned with God's glory than with his own legacy. He reminded God of His promises to Abraham, Isaac, and Jacob, and he argued that destroying the Israelites would bring dishonor to God's name among the nations. Moses understood that God's will was not just about the immediate situation, but also about upholding His honor and glory in the eyes of the world. This ability to see the bigger picture and to prioritize God's glory above all else is a key aspect of discernment. It shows that true discernment is not just about making the right decisions in the moment; it is also about understanding how those decisions impact God's reputation and honor.

Moses' ability to discern God's will also required him to have a deep sense of humility. Despite being chosen by God to lead the people of Israel, Moses did not let his position or authority go to his head. Instead, he remained humble and focused on doing what was right in the eyes of God. This humility is an important aspect of discernment, as it allows us to be open to God's guidance and to make decisions that are in line with His will, rather than our own desires or ambitions. Moses understood that his role as a leader was not about seeking power or recognition for himself, but about serving God and guiding the people in the way that they should go. This humility allowed him to discern God's will and to act in accordance with it, even when it was difficult or required personal sacrifice.

Moses' discernment of God's will also involved a deep sense of responsibility for the spiritual well-being of the people he was leading.

WHO IS ON THE LORD'S SIDE? A CALL TO RIGHTEOUSNESS

By drawing a line between those who were for God and those who were against Him, Moses was taking responsibility for guiding the people back to the right path. He understood that as their leader, it was his responsibility to ensure that the people were living in accordance with God's commands and that they were not led astray by sin or idolatry. This sense of responsibility is a crucial aspect of discernment, as it requires us to be willing to take on the difficult task of guiding others in the way of righteousness, even when it is challenging or unpopular.

Moses' ability to discern God's will also required him to be patient and to persevere in the face of adversity. The people of Israel were often disobedient, rebellious, and ungrateful, and they frequently questioned Moses' leadership. However, despite all of these challenges, Moses never gave up. He continued to seek God's guidance and to lead the people with patience and determination, even when the going was tough. This perseverance is an important aspect of discernment, as it requires us to stay the course and to continue seeking God's will, even when it is difficult or when we face opposition.

Moses' discernment of God's will also involved a deep understanding of the importance of obedience. Throughout his life, Moses was consistently obedient to God's commands, even when they were difficult or didn't make sense to him. Whether it was leading the people out of Egypt, crossing the Red Sea, or wandering in the wilderness for forty years, Moses trusted God and followed His instructions. This obedience is a key aspect of discernment, as it requires us to trust in God's plan and to follow His guidance, even when we don't fully understand it or when it requires us to make difficult decisions.

Moses' ability to discern God's will also involved a deep sense of compassion for the people he was leading. Despite their repeated disobedience and rebellion, Moses continued to care for the people and to seek their well-being. He was willing to stand in the gap for them, to intercede on their behalf, and to take on the difficult task of guiding them back to God. This compassion is a crucial aspect of discernment, as it requires us to be willing to put the needs of others above our own and to seek their well-being, even when it is difficult or challenging.

Moses' discernment of God's will also required him to be bold and courageous in his decisions. When he saw the people worshipping the golden calf, he did not hesitate to take decisive action to address the sin and to restore the people's relationship with God. This boldness is an important aspect of discernment, as it requires us to be willing to take action when necessary and to make difficult decisions in order to carry out God's will.

Moses' ability to discern God's will also involved a deep sense of responsibility for the people's relationship with God. He understood that as their leader, it was his responsibility to ensure that the people were living in accordance with God's commands and that they were not led astray by sin or idolatry. This sense of responsibility is a crucial aspect of discernment, as it requires us to be willing to take on the difficult task of guiding others in the way of righteousness, even when it is challenging or unpopular.

Moses' discernment of God's will also required him to be patient and to persevere in the face of adversity. The people of Israel were often disobedient, rebellious, and ungrateful, and they frequently questioned Moses' leadership. However, despite all of these challenges, Moses never gave up. He continued to seek God's guidance and to lead the people with patience and determination, even when the going was tough. This perseverance is an important aspect of discernment, as it requires us to stay the course and to continue seeking God's will, even when it is difficult or when we face opposition.

In conclusion, Moses' ability to discern God's will is a powerful example of what it means to lead with wisdom and courage. His decision to draw a line between those who were for God and those who were against Him reflects the deep discernment he had in understanding and carrying out God's will. Throughout his life, Moses consistently sought to follow God's guidance and to make decisions that were in line with His commands, even when those decisions were difficult or unpopular. His ability to discern God's will was not just about making the right decisions in the moment; it was also about understanding the deeper implications of those decisions and guiding the people in their ongoing relationship with God. Moses' life challenges us to seek God's will in all that we do, to be bold and courageous in our decisions, and to be willing to take responsibility for the outcomes of those decisions. His example shows us that true discernment requires humility, patience, perseverance, and a deep commitment to following God's guidance, even in the most complex and challenging situations.

Chapter 9 - Plea for Repentance

In the story of Moses and the golden calf, found in Exodus 32, we see a powerful example of the necessity of repentance and the critical role it plays in our relationship with God. The Israelites, who had been miraculously delivered from slavery in Egypt by God through Moses, found themselves in a moment of weakness and impatience. While Moses was on Mount Sinai receiving the Ten Commandments from God, the people grew restless and anxious, wondering what had become of him. In their impatience, they turned to Aaron, Moses' brother, and demanded that he make them a god to worship. Aaron, either out of fear or a desire to appease the people, gave in to their demands and created a golden calf from the gold jewelry the people had brought out of Egypt. The Israelites then began to worship this idol, proclaiming that it was the god who had brought them out of Egypt. This act of idolatry was a direct violation of the covenant they had made with God, particularly the first two commandments, which forbade the worship of other gods and the creation of idols. When Moses descended from the mountain and saw the people's actions, he was filled with righteous anger, but more importantly, he knew that something had to be done to restore the people to their rightful relationship with God. Moses understood that the first step in this process of restoration was repentance.

Moses' response to the situation was both decisive and powerful. He immediately took action to confront the sin that had taken hold of the camp. He shattered the stone tablets on which the Ten Commandments were written, symbolizing the broken covenant between God and the people. He then ground the golden calf into powder, scattered it on the water, and made the people drink it, a symbolic act meant to show them the futility and bitterness of their idolatry. However, Moses did not stop there. He knew that outward actions alone would not be enough to restore the people to a right relationship with God; what was needed was a change of heart, a turning away from sin, and a sincere return to God. This is where the call to repentance comes in.

By demanding a clear choice, Moses implicitly called the people to repentance. Standing at the gate of the camp, he called out, "Who is on the Lord's side? Let him come unto me." This was more than just a call to gather the faithful; it was a clear and unambiguous demand for the people to make a choice. They had to decide whether they would continue in their idolatry, worshipping the golden calf, or whether they would turn back to God, renouncing their sin and recommitting themselves to the covenant they had made with Him. This call to choose sides was, in essence, a call to repentance. It required the people to recognize their sin, to feel genuine sorrow for what they had done, and to make a deliberate decision to turn away from that sin and return to God. This is the essence of repentance: it is not just about feeling sorry for our actions, but about making a conscious decision to turn away from those actions and to seek reconciliation with God.

Moses understood that repentance was the first and most crucial step in returning to God. Without repentance, there could be no forgiveness, no restoration, and no renewal of the covenant. The people had to first acknowledge their sin, take responsibility for it, and then make a deliberate choice to turn away from it and return to God. This is why Moses' call was so urgent and so clear. He knew that the people's relationship with God was at stake, and he wanted them to understand that there was no middle ground, no room for compromise. They could not continue to worship the golden calf and still claim to be God's people. They had to make a clear and decisive choice, and that choice had to begin with repentance.

Repentance is a theme that runs throughout the Bible, and it is always presented as the first step in restoring our relationship with God. From the prophets of the Old Testament to the teachings of Jesus in the New Testament, the message is consistent: before we can be forgiven, before we can be restored, we must first repent. Repentance is the acknowledgment of our sin, the recognition that we have strayed from God's path, and the decision to turn away from that sin and return to God. It is a fundamental aspect of our faith, and it is something that we are called to do repeatedly throughout our lives. Just as the Israelites were called to repent of their idolatry and return to God, so too are we called to examine our own lives, to recognize where we have gone astray, and to turn back to God in repentance.

Moses' call to repentance also highlights the importance of making a clear and deliberate choice. Repentance is not something that happens by accident; it is a conscious decision that we must make. It requires us to take a hard look at our lives, to recognize where we have sinned, and to make a deliberate choice to turn away from that sin and to seek God's forgiveness. This is why Moses' call was so powerful. By demanding that the people choose sides, he was forcing them to confront their sin and to make a deliberate decision about what they were going to do about it. Were they going to continue in their idolatry, or were they going to repent and return to God? This is a decision that each of us must make in our own lives. We cannot continue to live in sin and still claim to be followers of God. We must make a deliberate choice to turn away from that sin and to seek God's forgiveness.

Moses' actions in this story also demonstrate the seriousness of sin and the importance of addressing it directly. He did not try to downplay the people's sin or to excuse their behavior. Instead, he confronted it head-on, taking decisive action to address the idolatry that had taken hold of the camp. This is an important lesson for us as well. When we recognize sin in our lives, we must be willing to confront it directly and to take decisive action to address it. Repentance is not just about feeling sorry for our sin; it is about taking responsibility for it and doing whatever it takes to turn away from it and to restore our relationship with God.

Moses' call to repentance also highlights the importance of accountability. By demanding that the people make a clear choice, he was holding them accountable for their actions. He was making it clear that there were consequences for their behavior and that they needed to take responsibility for what they had done. This is a crucial aspect of repentance. It is not enough to simply recognize our sin; we must also take responsibility for it and be willing to face the consequences of our actions. This is why Moses' call was so urgent and so clear. He wanted the people to understand that they could not continue to live in sin without facing the consequences. They had to take responsibility for their actions, repent, and seek God's forgiveness.

Moses' call to repentance also emphasizes the importance of sincerity in our relationship with God. Repentance is not just about going through the motions or saying the right words; it is about a genuine change of heart. It requires us to truly recognize the seriousness of our sin, to feel genuine sorrow for what we have done, and to make a sincere commitment to turn away from that sin and to live in a way that is pleasing to God. This is why Moses' call was so powerful. He was not just asking the people to say they were sorry; he was calling them to a genuine change of heart, a sincere repentance that would restore their relationship with God.

Moses' actions in this story also demonstrate the role of a leader in guiding others to repentance. As the leader of the Israelites, Moses took responsibility for addressing the sin in the camp and for guiding the people back to God. He did not shy away from this responsibility, even though it was difficult and uncomfortable. Instead, he confronted the people's sin directly and called them to repentance. This is an important lesson for all of us, especially for those in positions of leadership. As leaders, we have a responsibility to guide others in the way of righteousness and to call them to repentance when they have gone astray. This is not always an easy task, but it is a crucial aspect of spiritual leadership.

Moses' call to repentance also highlights the importance of obedience to God's commands. The people's sin was a direct violation of the covenant they had made with God, and their repentance was necessary in order to restore that covenant. Repentance requires us to recognize where we have disobeyed God's commands and to make a deliberate choice to turn away from that disobedience and to recommit ourselves to living in accordance with God's will. This is why Moses' call was so urgent. He knew that the people's relationship with God was at stake, and he wanted them to understand that they could not continue to live in disobedience without facing the consequences. They had to repent and recommit themselves to living in accordance with God's commands.

Moses' actions in this story also demonstrate the importance of intercession in the process of repentance. After confronting the people's sin and calling them to repentance, Moses went before God to plead for their forgiveness. He was willing to stand in the gap for the people, to intercede on their behalf, and to seek God's mercy and forgiveness for their sin. This is an important aspect of repentance. It requires us to not only recognize our sin and turn away from it, but also to seek God's forgiveness and to trust in His mercy. Moses' intercession on behalf of the people is a powerful example of the role of intercession in the process of repentance.

Moses' call to repentance also emphasizes the importance of renewal in our relationship with God. Repentance is not just about turning away from sin; it is also about turning back to God and renewing our commitment to Him. After the people had repented of their idolatry, Moses led them in renewing their covenant with God, reminding them of His commands and His promises. This renewal is a crucial aspect of repentance. It is not enough to simply turn away from sin; we must also turn back to God and recommit ourselves to living in accordance with His will. This is why Moses' call was so powerful.

He was not just calling the people to turn away from their sin; he was calling them to return to God and to renew their commitment to Him.

Moses' actions in this story also demonstrate the importance of perseverance in the process of repentance. The people of Israel were often disobedient, rebellious, and ungrateful, and they frequently strayed from the path that God had set for them. However, despite all of these challenges, Moses never gave up. He continued to lead the people with patience and determination, guiding them back to God and calling them to repentance whenever they went astray. This perseverance is a crucial aspect of repentance. It requires us to keep striving to live in accordance with God's will, even when we fall short or face challenges. Repentance is not a one-time event; it is an ongoing process that requires perseverance and determination.

Moses' call to repentance also highlights the importance of faith in the process of repentance. Repentance requires us to have faith in God's mercy and forgiveness, to trust that He will forgive our sins and restore our relationship with Him. This faith is a crucial aspect of repentance. It allows us to turn away from our sin with confidence, knowing that God is faithful and just to forgive us and to cleanse us from all unrighteousness. This is why Moses' call was so powerful. He was not just asking the people to turn away from their sin; he was calling them to have faith in God's mercy and to trust in His forgiveness. In conclusion, Moses' call to repentance in the story of the golden calf is a powerful example of the necessity of repentance in our relationship with God. By demanding a clear choice, Moses implicitly called the people to repentance, illustrating the importance of repentance as the first step in returning to God. His actions demonstrate the seriousness of sin, the importance of accountability, the need for a sincere change of heart, and the role of intercession and renewal in the process of repentance. Moses' life challenges us to examine our own lives, to recognize where we have gone astray, and to make a deliberate choice to turn away from our sin and to return to God in repentance. His example shows us that repentance is not just about feeling sorry for our actions; it is about making a conscious decision to turn away from those actions and to seek reconciliation with God. It is the first and most crucial step in restoring our relationship with God, and it is something that we are called to do repeatedly throughout our lives. Moses' call to repentance is a timeless reminder of the importance of turning away from sin and returning to God, and it challenges us to live lives of repentance, obedience, and faith.

Chapter 10 - Preparedness to Stand Alone

Moses is one of the most remarkable figures in the Bible, and his life offers many important lessons about leadership, faith, and the courage to stand alone in the face of overwhelming opposition. One of the most striking examples of this courage is found in the story of the golden calf in Exodus 32. The Israelites, who had been miraculously delivered from slavery in Egypt by God through Moses, found themselves in a moment of weakness and impatience. While Moses was on Mount Sinai receiving the Ten Commandments from God, the people grew restless and anxious, wondering what had become of him. In their impatience, they turned to Aaron, Moses' brother, and demanded that he make them a god to worship. Aaron, either out of fear or a desire to appease the people, gave in to their demands and created a golden calf from the gold jewelry the people had brought out of Egypt. The Israelites then began to worship this idol, proclaiming that it was the god who had brought them out of Egypt. This act of idolatry was a direct violation of the covenant they had made with God, particularly the first two commandments, which forbade the worship of other gods and the creation of idols. When Moses descended from the mountain and saw the people's actions, he was filled with righteous anger, but more importantly, he demonstrated a courage that few possess—the courage to stand alone for what is right, even when it means going against the crowd.

Moses could have easily chosen the path of least resistance. He could have returned to the camp and tried to reason with the people, to find a compromise that would appease their desires while still maintaining some semblance of faithfulness to God. He could have chosen to overlook their sin, hoping that they would eventually come to their senses on their own. But Moses knew that this was not an option. He understood that the people's actions were not just a minor lapse in judgment; they were a direct affront to the God who had delivered them from bondage, and they threatened to undermine the very foundation of the covenant that had been established between God and Israel. In this moment, Moses was faced with a choice: he could either go along with the crowd, joining them in their idolatry and disobedience, or he could stand alone, standing firm in his commitment to God, even if it meant facing the anger and rejection of the very people he had been called to lead.

Moses chose the latter. He chose to stand alone, to take a stand for what was right, even when it meant going against the crowd. He knew that true faithfulness to God required more than just going along with the majority; it required a willingness to stand firm in one's convictions, even when those convictions were unpopular or met with resistance. This is one of the most important lessons that we can learn from Moses' life: true faithfulness to God may require standing alone, even when it means going against the crowd. It requires a courage that is rooted not in the approval of others, but in a deep and abiding commitment to doing what is right in the eyes of God.

Moses' decision to stand alone in this moment was not just an act of defiance; it was an act of deep faith and trust in God. He knew that God had called him to lead the people out of Egypt and into the Promised Land, and he was determined to fulfill that calling, no matter what obstacles or challenges he faced along the way. He knew that God was faithful and that He would honor those who stood firm in their commitment to Him, even when it meant going against the crowd. This trust in God gave Moses the strength and courage to stand alone, to confront the people's sin directly, and to take the necessary steps to restore their relationship with God.

Moses' actions in this story also demonstrate the importance of integrity in leadership. He could have easily compromised his principles in order to maintain his position of authority or to avoid conflict with the people. But Moses understood that true leadership requires more than just maintaining power or popularity; it requires a commitment to doing what is right, even when it is difficult or unpopular. He knew that his first loyalty was to God, not to the opinions or desires of the people, and he was willing to stand alone in order to uphold that loyalty. This integrity is what set Moses apart as a leader and what made him such a powerful and effective servant of God.

Moses' courage to stand alone also highlights the importance of accountability in leadership. By confronting the people's sin and taking decisive action to address it, Moses was holding them accountable for their actions. He was making it clear that there were consequences for their behavior and that they needed to take responsibility for what they had done. This is a crucial aspect of leadership: the willingness to hold others accountable, even when it is difficult or unpopular. Moses understood that the people's relationship with God was at stake, and he was willing to stand alone in order to ensure that they understood the seriousness of their actions and the need for repentance.

Moses' decision to stand alone also required him to take responsibility for the spiritual well-being of the people he was leading. As their leader, he knew that it was his responsibility to guide them back to the right path when they went astray, even if it meant standing alone in doing so. This sense of responsibility is a key aspect of leadership, and it requires a willingness to take on the difficult task of guiding others in the way of righteousness, even when it is challenging or unpopular. Moses' actions in this moment demonstrate the importance of taking responsibility for the well-being of others, even when it requires standing alone.

Moses' courage to stand alone also involved a deep sense of humility. Despite being chosen by God to lead the people of Israel, Moses did not let his position or authority go to his head. Instead, he remained humble and focused on doing what was right in the eyes of God. This humility is an important aspect of courage, as it allows us to be open to God's guidance and to make decisions that are in line with His will, rather than our own desires or ambitions. Moses understood that his role as a leader was not about seeking power or recognition for himself, but about serving God and guiding the people in the way that they should go. This humility allowed him to stand alone with courage and conviction, even when it was difficult or required personal sacrifice.

Moses' decision to stand alone also required him to have a deep sense of compassion for the people he was leading. Despite their repeated disobedience and rebellion, Moses continued to care for the people and to seek their well-being. He was willing to stand in the gap for them, to intercede on their behalf, and to take on the difficult task of guiding them back to God. This compassion is a crucial aspect of courage, as it requires us to be willing to put the needs of others above our own and to seek their well-being, even when it is difficult or challenging. Moses' actions in this moment show that true courage is not just about standing firm in one's convictions, but also about caring for others and seeking their well-being, even when it requires standing alone.

Moses' courage to stand alone also involved a deep sense of perseverance. The people of Israel were often disobedient, rebellious, and ungrateful, and they frequently questioned Moses' leadership. However, despite all of these challenges, Moses never gave up. He continued to lead the people with patience and determination, guiding them back to God and calling them to repentance whenever they went astray. This perseverance is a crucial aspect of courage, as it requires us to keep striving to live in accordance with God's will, even when we fall short or face challenges. Moses' perseverance in the face of the people's disobedience is a powerful example of what it means to have true courage.

Moses' decision to stand alone also required him to have a deep faith in God's promises. He knew that God had called him to lead the people out of Egypt and into the Promised Land, and he trusted that God would fulfill that promise, even when the journey was difficult or when the people were disobedient. This faith gave Moses the strength and courage to stand alone, to confront the people's sin, and to take the necessary steps to restore their relationship with God. This trust in God is a key aspect of courage, as it allows us to stand firm in our convictions, even when we face opposition or when the path ahead is uncertain.

Moses' courage to stand alone also highlights the importance of obedience in our relationship with God. Throughout his life, Moses was consistently obedient to God's commands, even when they were difficult or didn't make sense to him. Whether it was leading the people out of Egypt, crossing the Red Sea, or wandering in the wilderness for forty years, Moses trusted God and followed His instructions. This obedience is a key aspect of courage, as it requires us to trust in God's plan and to follow His guidance, even when it requires us to make difficult decisions or to stand alone in the face of opposition.

Moses' decision to stand alone also required him to be bold and courageous in his decisions. When he saw the people worshipping the golden calf, he did not hesitate to take decisive action to address the sin and to restore the people's relationship with God. This boldness is an important aspect of courage, as it requires us to be willing to take action when necessary and to make difficult decisions in order to carry out God's will. Moses' boldness in standing alone and confronting the people's sin is a powerful example of what it means to have true courage.

Moses' courage to stand alone also involved a deep sense of responsibility for the people's relationship with God. He understood that as their leader, it was his responsibility to ensure that the people were living in accordance with God's commands and that they were not led astray by sin or idolatry. This sense of responsibility is a crucial aspect of courage, as it requires us to be willing to take on the difficult task of guiding others in the way of righteousness, even when it is challenging or unpopular.

Moses' courage to stand alone also involved a deep understanding of the importance of God's honor and glory. When God threatened to destroy the Israelites and start over with Moses, making him the father of a new nation, Moses could have easily accepted this offer and elevated his own status. However, Moses was more concerned with God's glory than with his own legacy. He reminded God of His promises to Abraham, Isaac, and Jacob, and he argued that destroying the Israelites would bring dishonor to God's name among the nations. Moses understood that God's will was not just about the immediate situation, but also about upholding His honor and glory in the eyes of the world. This ability to see the bigger picture and to prioritize God's glory above all else is a key aspect of courage. It shows that true courage is not just about making the right decisions in the moment; it is also about understanding how those decisions impact God's reputation and honor.

Moses' courage to stand alone also involved a deep sense of humility. Despite being chosen by God to lead the people of Israel, Moses did not let his position go to his head. Instead, he remained humble and focused on doing what was right in the eyes of God. This humility is an important aspect of courage, as it allows us to be open to God's guidance and to make decisions that are in line with His will, rather than our own desires or ambitions. Moses understood that his role as a leader was not about seeking power or recognition for himself, but about serving God and guiding the people in the way that they should go. This humility allowed him to stand alone with courage and conviction, even when it was difficult or required personal sacrifice.

Moses' decision to stand alone also required him to have a deep sense of compassion for the people he was leading. Despite their repeated disobedience and rebellion, Moses continued to care for the people and to seek their well-being. He was willing to stand in the gap for them, to intercede on their behalf, and to take on the difficult task of guiding them back to God. This compassion is a crucial aspect of courage, as it requires us to be willing to put the needs of others above our own and to seek their well-being, even when it is difficult or challenging.

Moses' courage to stand alone also involved a deep sense of perseverance. The people of Israel were often disobedient, rebellious, and ungrateful, and they frequently questioned Moses' leadership. However, despite all of these challenges, Moses never gave up. He continued to lead the people with patience and determination, guiding them back to God and calling them to repentance whenever they went astray. This perseverance is a crucial aspect of courage, as it requires us to keep striving to live in accordance with God's will, even when we fall short or face challenges. Moses' perseverance in the face of the people's disobedience is a powerful example of what it means to have true courage.

In conclusion, Moses' courage to stand alone in the story of the golden calf is a powerful example of what it means to have true faithfulness to God. His willingness to stand firm in his convictions, even when it meant going against the crowd, demonstrates the importance of courage, integrity, accountability, responsibility, humility, compassion, perseverance, faith, and obedience in our relationship with God. Moses' life challenges us to examine our own lives and to ask ourselves whether we are willing to stand alone for what is right, even when it is difficult or unpopular. His example shows us that true courage is not about seeking the approval of others, but about standing firm in our commitment to God, no matter the cost. It is a powerful reminder that true faithfulness to God may require us to stand alone, to take a stand for what is right, and to trust in God's guidance and strength, even in the face of overwhelming opposition.

Chapter 11 - Positioning Leadership in God's Authority

Moses is one of the most prominent figures in the Bible, and his life serves as a profound example of leadership that is rooted not in personal power or ambition, but in the authority that comes from a deep and genuine relationship with God. Throughout his life, Moses was called upon to lead the people of Israel through some of the most challenging and transformative moments in their history, from their liberation from slavery in Egypt to their journey through the wilderness to the brink of the Promised Land. One of the most powerful and instructive moments in Moses' leadership is found in the story of the golden calf in Exodus 32. While Moses was on Mount Sinai receiving the Ten Commandments from God, the people of Israel grew restless and anxious. In his absence, they pressured Aaron, Moses' brother, to create a god they could worship, leading to the construction of a golden calf. The people then began to worship this idol, proclaiming that it was the god who had brought them out of Egypt. This act of idolatry was a direct violation of the covenant they had made with God, and it threatened to destroy the very foundation of their relationship with Him. When Moses descended from the mountain and saw what the people were doing, he was faced with a situation that required not only decisive action but also a deep understanding of the authority he held as a leader. His response to this crisis reveals that his authority was not based on personal power or charisma, but on his relationship with God and the divine authority that flowed from that relationship.

Moses' authority to call the people back to God's side, to demand repentance, and to take decisive action in the face of their sin was rooted in his deep and abiding relationship with God. Throughout his life, Moses consistently sought God's guidance and direction, whether in moments of triumph or in the face of seemingly insurmountable challenges. He did not rely on his own strength or wisdom; instead, he leaned on God, trusting that it was God's power, not his own, that would sustain him and enable him to fulfill his calling. This reliance on God's authority is what gave Moses the confidence to stand before Pharaoh and demand the release of the Israelites, to lead the people through the Red Sea, and to guide them through the wilderness. It is also what gave him the courage to confront the people's sin directly when they turned to idolatry in his absence.

When Moses came down from Mount Sinai and saw the people worshiping the golden calf, he did not hesitate to take action. He knew that their sin was not just a minor transgression, but a direct affront to the God who had delivered them from slavery and had made a covenant with them. In this moment, Moses did not act out of personal anger or a desire to assert his own authority; rather, he acted out of a deep sense of responsibility to uphold God's authority and to restore the people to a right relationship with Him. He understood that his role as a leader was not to seek power for himself, but to be a steward of the authority that God had entrusted to him. This is what true spiritual leadership looks like: it is leadership that is rooted not in personal ambition, but in a deep and abiding relationship with God and a commitment to carrying out His will.

Moses' actions in this moment also highlight the importance of humility in leadership. Despite being chosen by God to lead the people of Israel, Moses did not let his position or authority go to his head. Instead, he remained humble, recognizing that his authority came not from himself, but from God. This humility allowed Moses to lead with integrity, always seeking to do what was right in the eyes of God, rather than seeking to please the people or to assert his own power. It also allowed him to be open to God's guidance, to seek His wisdom in difficult situations, and to trust that God would provide the strength and direction needed to lead the people through the challenges they faced. This is a crucial aspect of spiritual leadership: the recognition that true authority comes not from our own abilities or accomplishments, but from our relationship with God and our willingness to submit to His will.

Moses' authority to lead the people and to call them to repentance was also rooted in his deep sense of accountability to God. He understood that as a leader, he was accountable not just to the people, but ultimately to God. This sense of accountability drove him to take decisive action in the face of the people's sin, knowing that he would one day have to stand before God and give an account for how he had led the people. This is a key aspect of spiritual leadership: the recognition that we are accountable to God for how we lead, and the willingness to take responsibility for the spiritual well-being of those we are called to lead. Moses' actions in this moment demonstrate the importance of taking this responsibility seriously, even when it requires making difficult decisions or standing alone in the face of opposition.

Moses' relationship with God also gave him the discernment needed to understand the deeper implications of the people's sin and the steps that were needed to restore their relationship with God. He did not simply react out of anger or frustration; instead, he sought to understand what God's will was in the situation and how he could best lead the people back to a place of faithfulness and obedience. This discernment is another key aspect of spiritual leadership: the ability to seek God's guidance in complex situations and to make decisions that are in line with His will. Moses' actions in this moment demonstrate that true leadership requires more than just making the right decisions; it requires a deep understanding of God's will and a commitment to carrying out that will, even when it is difficult or unpopular.

Moses' authority to lead was also strengthened by the trust and respect he had earned from the people over time. While the people did not always agree with his decisions or follow his leadership perfectly, they knew that Moses was a man of integrity who was committed to their well-being and to following God's guidance. This trust was not something that Moses had demanded or coerced from the people; it was something that he had earned through his consistent faithfulness, humility, and dedication to God's will. This is an important lesson for all leaders: true authority is not something that can be imposed from above; it is something that must be earned through consistent, faithful, and humble leadership that is rooted in a deep relationship with God.

Moses' authority to lead also came from his willingness to intercede for the people when they had gone astray. After confronting the people's sin and calling them to repentance, Moses went before God to plead for their forgiveness. He was willing to stand in the gap for the people, to take on the burden of their sin, and to seek God's mercy on their behalf. This willingness to intercede for those we lead is another key aspect of spiritual leadership. It requires us to be willing to carry the burdens of others, to seek God's mercy and guidance on their behalf, and to stand with them in their struggles and challenges. Moses' actions in this moment demonstrate that true leadership is not just about making decisions or asserting authority; it is about caring for those we lead and being willing to stand with them in their moments of weakness and failure.

Moses' authority to lead was also rooted in his obedience to God's commands. Throughout his life, Moses was consistently obedient to God, even when His commands were difficult or didn't make sense to him. Whether it was leading the people out of Egypt, crossing the Red Sea, or wandering in the wilderness for forty years, Moses trusted God and followed His instructions. This obedience is a key aspect of spiritual leadership, as it requires us to trust in God's plan and to follow His guidance, even when it requires us to make difficult decisions or to stand alone in the face of opposition. Moses' obedience to God's commands is a powerful example of what it means to be a leader who is rooted in God's authority, rather than in personal power or ambition.

Moses' authority to lead also came from his deep sense of compassion for the people he was leading. Despite their repeated disobedience and rebellion, Moses continued to care for the people and to seek their well-being. He was willing to stand in the gap for them, to intercede on their behalf, and to take on the difficult task of guiding them back to God. This compassion is a crucial aspect of spiritual leadership, as it requires us to be willing to put the needs of others above our own and to seek their well-being, even when it is difficult or challenging. Moses' actions in this moment show that true leadership is not just about asserting authority or making decisions; it is about caring for those we lead and seeking their well-being, even when it requires personal sacrifice.

Moses' authority to lead was also rooted in his perseverance in the face of adversity. The people of Israel were often disobedient, rebellious, and ungrateful, and they frequently questioned Moses' leadership. However, despite all of these challenges, Moses never gave up. He continued to lead the people with patience and determination, guiding them back to God and calling them to repentance whenever they went astray. This perseverance is a crucial aspect of spiritual leadership, as it requires us to keep striving to live in accordance with God's will, even when we face challenges or opposition. Moses' perseverance in the face of the people's disobedience is a powerful example of what it means to be a leader who is rooted in God's authority and committed to carrying out His will, no matter the cost.

Moses' authority to lead also involved a deep understanding of the importance of God's honor and glory. When God threatened to destroy the Israelites and start over with Moses, making him the father of a new nation, Moses could have easily accepted this offer and elevated his own status. However, Moses was more concerned with God's glory than with his own legacy. He reminded God of His promises to Abraham, Isaac, and Jacob, and he argued that destroying the Israelites would bring dishonor to God's name among the nations. Moses understood that God's will was not just about the immediate situation, but also about upholding His honor and glory in the eyes of the world. This ability to see the bigger picture and to prioritize God's glory above all else is a key aspect of spiritual leadership. It shows that true leadership is not just about making the right decisions in the moment; it is also about understanding how those decisions impact God's reputation and honor.

Moses' authority to lead was also rooted in his deep sense of responsibility for the people's relationship with God. He understood that as their leader, it was his responsibility to ensure that the people were living in accordance with God's commands and that they were not led astray by sin or idolatry. This sense of responsibility is a crucial aspect of spiritual leadership, as it requires us to be willing to take on the difficult task of guiding others in the way of righteousness, even when it is challenging or unpopular. Moses' actions in this moment demonstrate the importance of taking this responsibility seriously, even when it requires making difficult decisions or standing alone in the face of opposition.

Moses' authority to lead was also strengthened by the trust and respect he had earned from the people over time. While the people did not always agree with his decisions or follow his leadership perfectly, they knew that Moses was a man of integrity who was committed to their well-being and to following God's guidance. This trust was not something that Moses had demanded or coerced from the people; it was something that he had earned through his consistent faithfulness, humility, and dedication to God's will. This is an important lesson for all leaders: true authority is not something that can be imposed from above; it is something that must be earned through consistent, faithful, and humble leadership that is rooted in a deep relationship with God.

In conclusion, Moses' authority to lead the people of Israel was not based on personal power or ambition, but on his deep and abiding relationship with God. His authority to call the people to God's side, to demand repentance, and to take decisive action in the face of their sin was rooted in his understanding that true spiritual leadership must be based on God's authority rather than personal power. Throughout his life, Moses demonstrated the qualities of a true spiritual leader: humility, accountability, obedience, compassion, perseverance, and a deep commitment to God's will. His life challenges us to examine our own leadership and to ask ourselves whether our authority is rooted in our relationship with God or in our own desires for power or recognition. Moses' example shows us that true leadership is not about asserting authority or seeking power for ourselves; it is about being a steward of the authority that God has entrusted to us, leading with humility, integrity, and a deep commitment to doing what is right in the eyes of God. It is a powerful reminder that true spiritual leadership is not about us; it is about pointing others to God and leading them in a way that brings honor and glory to His name.

Chapter 12 - Pledge to Justice and Righteousness

Moses is one of the most significant figures in the Bible, and his life provides numerous lessons about leadership, faith, and the unwavering commitment to justice and righteousness that is required of those who seek to lead God's people. Among the many episodes in Moses' life that illustrate these principles, the story of the golden calf in Exodus 32 stands out as a powerful example of how godly leadership involves upholding justice and righteousness, even when it requires making difficult and unpopular decisions. The Israelites, who had been miraculously delivered from slavery in Egypt by God through Moses, found themselves in a moment of weakness and impatience. While Moses was on Mount Sinai receiving the Ten Commandments from God, the people grew restless and anxious, wondering what had become of him. In their impatience, they turned to Aaron, Moses' brother, and demanded that he make them a god to worship. Aaron, either out of fear or a desire to appease the people, gave in to their demands and created a golden calf from the gold jewelry the people had brought out of Egypt. The Israelites then began to worship this idol, proclaiming that it was the god who had brought them out of Egypt. This act of idolatry was a direct violation of the covenant they had made with God, particularly the first two commandments, which forbade the worship of other gods and the creation of idols. When Moses descended from the mountain and saw the people's actions, he was faced with a situation that required not only decisive action but also a deep understanding of the principles of justice and righteousness that he was called to uphold as the leader of God's people.

Moses' response to this crisis was rooted in his unwavering commitment to justice and righteousness, values that are central to godly leadership. He understood that the people's actions were not just a minor lapse in judgment; they were a serious breach of the covenant they had made with God, and they threatened to undermine the very foundation of their relationship with Him. In this moment, Moses knew that he could not simply overlook the people's sin or try to appease them by finding a compromise that would allow them to continue in their idolatry while still claiming to be followers of God. Instead, he recognized that justice and righteousness demanded that the people be held accountable for their actions, and that steps be taken to restore their relationship with God. This is one of the most important lessons that we can learn from Moses' life: true godly leadership involves a commitment to upholding justice and righteousness, even when it requires making difficult decisions or taking actions that may be unpopular or met with resistance.

Moses' actions in response to the people's idolatry were both decisive and rooted in a deep sense of justice and righteousness. Upon seeing the golden calf and the people's worship of it, Moses did not hesitate to take action. He shattered the stone tablets on which the Ten Commandments were written, symbolizing the broken covenant between God and the people. He then ground the golden calf into powder, scattered it on the water, and made the people drink it, a symbolic act meant to show them the futility and bitterness of their idolatry. However, Moses did not stop there. He knew that the people's sin could not simply be swept under the rug or dealt with through symbolic actions alone; true justice and righteousness required that the people be called to account for their actions and that those who refused to repent be dealt with accordingly. To this end, Moses called for those who were on the Lord's side to come to him, and the Levites responded. He then instructed the Levites to go through the camp and execute judgment on those who had refused to repent of their idolatry. This was a harsh and difficult task, but Moses knew that it was necessary in order to restore justice and righteousness among the people and to renew their covenant with God.

This episode highlights the importance of accountability in the pursuit of justice and righteousness. Moses understood that as a leader, he was responsible for ensuring that the people lived in accordance with God's commands, and that those who violated those commands were held accountable for their actions. This is a crucial aspect of godly leadership: the willingness to hold others accountable, even when it is difficult or uncomfortable. Moses knew that the people's relationship with God was at stake, and he was willing to make the difficult decisions necessary to restore that relationship, even if it meant standing alone or facing the anger and rejection of the people he was called to lead. This is what true commitment to justice and righteousness looks like: it is a commitment that is not swayed by the opinions or desires of others, but is rooted in a deep understanding of God's standards and a willingness to uphold those standards, no matter the cost.

Moses' commitment to justice and righteousness was also evident in his willingness to take responsibility for the spiritual well-being of the people he was leading. He understood that as their leader, it was his responsibility to guide them back to the right path when they went astray, even if it meant making difficult decisions or taking actions that were unpopular. This sense of responsibility is a key aspect of godly leadership, and it requires a willingness to take on the difficult task of guiding others in the way of righteousness, even when it is challenging or unpopular. Moses' actions in this moment demonstrate the importance of taking this responsibility seriously, and of being willing to make the difficult decisions necessary to uphold justice and righteousness, even when it requires personal sacrifice or standing alone in the face of opposition.

Moses' commitment to justice and righteousness was also rooted in his deep sense of humility and his understanding that true authority comes from God, not from personal power or ambition. Despite being chosen by God to lead the people of Israel, Moses did not let his position or authority go to his head. Instead, he remained humble, recognizing that his authority came not from himself, but from God. This humility allowed Moses to lead with integrity, always seeking to do what was right in the eyes of God, rather than seeking to please the people or to assert his own power. It also allowed him to be open to God's guidance, to seek His wisdom in difficult situations, and to trust that God would provide the strength and direction needed to lead the people through the challenges they faced. This is a crucial aspect of godly leadership: the recognition that true authority comes not from our own abilities or accomplishments, but from our relationship with God and our willingness to submit to His will.

Moses' commitment to justice and righteousness also involved a deep sense of compassion for the people he was leading. Despite their repeated disobedience and rebellion, Moses continued to care for the people and to seek their well-being. He was willing to stand in the gap for them, to intercede on their behalf, and to take on the difficult task of guiding them back to God. This compassion is a crucial aspect of godly leadership, as it requires us to be willing to put the needs of others above our own and to seek their well-being, even when it is difficult or challenging. Moses' actions in this moment show that true commitment to justice and righteousness is not just about enforcing rules or making difficult decisions; it is also about caring for those we lead and seeking their well-being, even when it requires personal sacrifice.

Moses' commitment to justice and righteousness was also evident in his perseverance in the face of adversity. The people of Israel were often disobedient, rebellious, and ungrateful, and they frequently questioned Moses' leadership. However, despite all of these challenges, Moses never gave up. He continued to lead the people with patience and determination, guiding them back to God and calling them to repentance whenever they went astray. This perseverance is a crucial aspect of godly leadership, as it requires us to keep striving to live in accordance with God's will, even when we face challenges or opposition. Moses' perseverance in the face of the people's disobedience is a powerful example of what it means to be a leader who is committed to justice and righteousness, no matter the cost.

Moses' commitment to justice and righteousness was also rooted in his deep understanding of the importance of God's honor and glory. When God threatened to destroy the Israelites and start over with Moses, making him the father of a new nation, Moses could have easily accepted this offer and elevated his own status. However, Moses was more concerned with God's glory than with his own legacy. He reminded God of His promises to Abraham, Isaac, and Jacob, and he argued that destroying the Israelites would bring dishonor to God's name among the nations. Moses understood that God's will was not just about the immediate situation, but also about upholding His honor and glory in the eyes of the world. This ability to see the bigger picture and to prioritize God's glory above all else is a key aspect of godly leadership. It shows that true leadership is not just about making the right decisions in the moment; it is also about understanding how those decisions impact God's reputation and honor, and being willing to make the difficult decisions necessary to uphold justice and righteousness, even when it is unpopular or met with resistance.

Moses' commitment to justice and righteousness also involved a deep sense of responsibility for the people's relationship with God. He understood that as their leader, it was his responsibility to ensure that the people were living in accordance with God's commands and that they were not led astray by sin or idolatry. This sense of responsibility is a crucial aspect of godly leadership, as it requires us to be willing to take on the difficult task of guiding others in the way of righteousness, even when it is challenging or unpopular. Moses' actions in this moment demonstrate the importance of taking this responsibility seriously, and of being willing to make the difficult decisions necessary to uphold justice and righteousness, even when it requires personal sacrifice or standing alone in the face of opposition.

Moses' commitment to justice and righteousness was also strengthened by the trust and respect he had earned from the people over time. While the people did not always agree with his decisions or follow his leadership perfectly, they knew that Moses was a man of integrity who was committed to their well-being and to following God's guidance. This trust was not something that Moses had demanded or coerced from the people; it was something that he had earned through his consistent faithfulness, humility, and dedication to God's will. This is an important lesson for all leaders: true authority is not something that can be imposed from above; it is something that must be earned through consistent, faithful, and humble leadership that is rooted in a deep relationship with God and a commitment to upholding justice and righteousness.

In conclusion, Moses' life is a powerful example of what it means to be a leader who is committed to justice and righteousness. His actions in response to the people's idolatry in Exodus 32 demonstrate that true godly leadership involves upholding these values, even when it requires making difficult and unpopular decisions. Moses' commitment to justice and righteousness was rooted in his deep relationship with God, his sense of accountability to God, his humility, his compassion for the people, his perseverance in the face of adversity, and his understanding of the importance of God's honor and glory. His life challenges us to examine our own leadership and to ask ourselves whether we are willing to make the difficult decisions necessary to uphold justice and righteousness, even when it requires personal sacrifice or standing alone in the face of opposition. Moses' example shows us that true leadership is not about seeking power or recognition for ourselves; it is about being a steward of the authority that God has entrusted to us, leading with humility, integrity, and a deep commitment to doing what is right in the eyes of God. It is a powerful reminder that true godly leadership is not about us; it is about pointing others to God and leading them in a way that brings honor and glory to His name, and that upholds the values of justice and righteousness that are at the heart of His character.

Conclusion

As we come to the end of "Who Is on the Lord's Side? A Call to Righteousness," it is essential to recognize that the principles and lessons explored throughout this book are not just historical reflections or theoretical ideas. They are practical, urgent calls to action for each of us in the days in which we live. The challenges we face—whether in our personal lives, our communities, or the broader society—require us to take a stand, to lead with integrity, and to call others to a path of righteousness that is anchored in the unchanging truth of God's Word.

The story of Moses standing at the gate of the camp, challenging the Israelites to declare their allegiance, is more relevant today than ever. It underscores the necessity of making a clear and unwavering choice in the face of moral and spiritual ambiguity. The principles drawn from Moses' leadership—boldness in crisis, commitment to God, moral courage, and a passion for righteousness—serve as a powerful framework for anyone who desires to make a difference in this world. These principles are not merely for leaders in positions of power; they are for every believer who seeks to live a life that honors God.

The question, "Who is on the Lord's side?" is not a one-time challenge but a daily call to examine where we stand in our relationship with God and in our response to the world around us. In an era marked by moral relativism and spiritual apathy, it is easy to be swayed by the shifting tides of cultural norms and societal pressures. Yet, as this book has emphasized, true leadership—whether in our homes, churches, or workplaces—requires us to stand firm in our convictions, even when it means standing alone. It requires us to uphold justice and righteousness, to speak the truth in love, and to lead others by example.

WHO IS ON THE LORD'S SIDE? A CALL TO RIGHTEOUSNESS

As we move forward, the challenge is clear: we must not be passive spectators in the face of moral decline or spiritual compromise. Instead, we must be active participants in God's work, leading others toward righteousness and truth. This requires a deep commitment to personal integrity, a willingness to confront sin and injustice, and a resolve to live out the principles of godly leadership in every aspect of our lives.

The journey ahead will not be easy. There will be moments of doubt, opposition, and temptation to compromise. But as Moses demonstrated, when our leadership is rooted in God's authority and our actions are guided by His principles, we can face these challenges with confidence and courage. The legacy we leave will not be one of fleeting success or popularity, but of lasting impact for God's kingdom.

As you close this book, I encourage you to take the lessons learned and apply them with renewed determination. Seek God's guidance daily, stand firm in your faith, and lead others with the same passion and commitment that Moses exemplified. The world desperately needs leaders who are willing to stand on the Lord's side, to call others to righteousness, and to live out the values of justice and integrity in every sphere of influence.

The question remains: Who is on the Lord's side? As you continue your journey, let your life be a resounding answer to that call—an answer that inspires others to stand with you in pursuit of God's righteousness and truth. The time to lead, to stand firm, and to call others to righteousness is now. The future depends on the choices we make today. Let us choose to stand on the Lord's side, no matter the cost.

Don't miss out!

Visit the website below and you can sign up to receive emails whenever Joshua Rhoades publishes a new book. There's no charge and no obligation.

https://books2read.com/r/B-A-AJLBB-FMPUE

BOOKS 2 READ

Connecting independent readers to independent writers.

Did you love *Who Is on the Lord's Side? A Call to Righteousness*? Then you should read *Renewed Hope- How to Find Encouragement in God*[1] by Joshua Rhoades!

[2]

In a world where challenges and hardships seem to come at us from every side, it's easy to feel overwhelmed, discouraged, and even hopeless. We all face moments when we wonder how we will ever make it through the difficulties we encounter. But in these times, the Bible offers us a powerful example of finding strength and hope, no matter the circumstances. In 1 Samuel 30:6, we read about David, a man who faced great trials and overwhelming odds, yet in the midst of it all, "David encouraged himself in the LORD his God." This simple yet profound statement serves as the foundation for this book, "Renewed Hope- How to Find Encouragement in God." David's life was filled with ups and downs, moments of triumph and times of deep despair. He knew what it was like to be pursued by enemies, to experience loss, and to feel abandoned. Yet, even in his darkest hours, David found a way to renew his hope by turning to God. He didn't rely on his own strength or seek comfort in worldly solutions. Instead, he looked to the LORD, drawing strength and encouragement from his relationship

---

1. https://books2read.com/u/boeko1

2. https://books2read.com/u/boeko1

with God. This book is an invitation to explore how we, too, can find renewed hope and encouragement in God, just as David did. It is a guide to understanding the power of faith, prayer, and trusting in God's promises, even when life seems unbearable. Throughout these pages, we will explore practical ways to draw closer to God, to encourage ourselves in Him, and to discover the peace and strength that come from relying on the LORD. Whether you are facing a specific challenge right now or simply want to deepen your relationship with God, this book will provide you with the tools and inspiration you need to find encouragement in the LORD. As we journey together through the principles found in David's example, you will learn how to shift your focus from the problems that surround you to the God who sustains you. You will discover that no matter what life throws at you, there is always hope in the LORD, and by encouraging yourself in Him, you can face any situation with renewed strength and confidence. This is not just a book about surviving difficult times, but about thriving through them by finding your hope and encouragement in the unchanging character of God. So, whether you are struggling with personal challenges, feeling weighed down by the burdens of life, or simply seeking a deeper sense of peace and purpose, "Renewed Hope-How to Find Encouragement in God" is here to remind you that you are not alone, and that with God, there is always a reason to hope. Let David's example inspire you to turn to the LORD, to find your strength in Him, and to walk forward with a renewed sense of hope, no matter what you face.